KNOWLEDGE AND COMPUTING

KNOWLEDGE AND COMPUTING

A COURSE ON COMPUTER EPISTEMOLOGY

TIBOR VÁMOS

CEU PRESS

Central European University Press
Budapest–New York

© 2010 by Tibor Vámos

Published in 2010 by

Central European University Press

An imprint of the
Central European University Share Company
Nádor utca 11, H-1051 Budapest, Hungary
Tel: +36-1-327-3138 or 327-3000
Fax: +36-1-327-3183
E-mail: ceupress@ceu.hu
Website: www.ceupress.com

400 West 59th Street, New York NY 10019, USA
Tel: +1-212-547-6932
Fax: +1-646-557-2416
E-mail: mgreenwald@sorosny.org

ISBN 978-963-9776-64-7 cloth

LIBRARY OF CONGRESS CATALOGING-IN-PUBLICATION DATA

Vámos, Tibor.
  Knowledge and computing : a course on computer epistemology / Tibor Vámos.
    p. cm.
  Includes bibliographical references and index.
  ISBN 978-9639776647 (hardcover)
1. Computer science. 2. Expert systems (Computer science) 3. Artificial intel-
ligence. I. Title.

  QA76.V326 2010
  006.3--dc22

2009051870

Printed in Hungary by
Akadémiai Nyomda, Martonvásár

Table of Contents

Dedicated to Dimitris Chorafas, who stimulated my original course on computer epistemology many years ago and created a secure background for me and for many people later on with his highly generous foundation.

Acknowledgements

Ferenc Bródy, József Bokor, Márta Fehér, Lajos Rónyai, János Gertler who read the drafts carefully and supported them with important comments, ideas, and goodwill but should not take responsibility for this final undertaking;
Édua Szűcs, the empathetic author of the cartoons;
Éva Nóra Nagy, who helped me smooth out my Hungarian-like English;
Gyöngyi Hetényi, in composition of the indexes and references;
Ágnes Koczka in composition of the figures.

On behalf of the publisher: Ms. Linda Kunos for her caretaking of the process, John Steinmetz for improving the style, and Károly Pavela for the page setting.

Lastly, my home away from home, the Computer and Automation Institute of the Hungarian Academy of Sciences, which tolerated this work, it being my hobby.

Preface of *Computer Epistemology*

This book is neither a textbook nor a monograph, but an essay. The style is defined by the subject and the objective. The subject matter lies in an area between computer science and philosophy, while the objective is to offer something between a general overview and practical advice. An essay is the form best suited for a work of this intermediate nature.

The thoughts presented here are the results of extensive practical experience: a decade in computer process control using large scale systems, another decade in machine pattern-recognition for vision systems, and nearly a decade dealing with artificial intelligence and expert systems. These real-life projects have taught me a critical appreciation of and respect for both abstract theory and the practical methodology that grows out of—and, in turn, shapes—those theories. As I dealt with the basic problems of large-scale systems modeling and control, my professional career—although seemingly diverse to an observer—led to this balanced view of the pros and cons of theory and practice.

From that perspective, this essay can be read as a philosophical reflection on large scale systems' practice, but this mirror also works in the opposite direction as well, as do most of our meditations. That is a natural aspect of any approach to the unreachable. Studying the philosophical background, nowadays mostly forgotten in the literature of artificial intelligence, I could find practically all the most recent technical ideas, presented more or less clearly, as far back as Greek Antiquity. As will be discussed in further detail, the flourishing of Greek philosophy around the 3rd century BCE, Medieval Science, especially the British schools of the 12-14th century, and the Age of Reason in the 17-18th century, have all contributed tremendously to those ideas about truth and falsity on which we now base our computer algorithms. This discovery was another lesson in modesty, and a further incentive to reach back as far as possible in the history of human thinking. Often the *process* of progress, the stories of unanswered questions, are as instructive as the phylogenetic processes of evolution. Nevertheless, as an essay this book is not intended as a survey of philosophy. It uses only those citations which were found to fit the essence of what I wanted to say. That essence is really the balanced viewpoint I described above.

The twentieth century has been filled with great, messianic promises and equally profound disappointments. This has happened not only in politics, economics, and technology, but can also be seen in the rapid changes and controversial directions of various arts. This was not the only century to claim first place in many aspects of life. As we have learned in systems science, non-linear behavior leads to chaotic disorder, and can reach new equilibria only by going through excessive perturbations.

One major vehicle of the twentieth century's technological progress is computer science. At its heart lie those efforts which could be modestly characterized as automated support for human work, but are more commonly known as *artificial intelligence*. All kinds of extreme views and perspectives on AI can be found in the literature, both in philosophy and computer science, but also in sociology, psychology and science fiction as well. This essay should be seen as a contribution to this on-going discussion, one that consists of both experience and insight, as described above.

For whom is this book written? Textbooks are written for students or those who would like to become acquainted with another field of knowledge related to their own work. Monographs are usually intended for a close circle of those who have special expertise; popular books aim for a very broad audience interested in some exciting new topic. An essay is written first for the author, as a device for organization and clarification of his own *Weltanschauung*. In the closest circle around this narcissistic center are those who have had similar thoughts and experiences, and the essay can be helpful to them in the further organization and clarification of these shared concerns. The next circle of the audience includes all those who have some professional interest in the topic as developers, users, or others concerned in some way. This determines the core content: a progressive, optimistic, appreciative, but critical view of the achievements and perspectives of our technology (modestly, I use the term *technology* here instead of *science*). If we would look for an attribute in the macrosphere, it is the traditional liberal-humanistic view. Winking at those circles, the reader finds an explanation of the confused usage of pronominal forms: I, we, somebody, anybody, etc. *We* will return to that in the conclusion.

The prior knowledge required is a fuzzy concept as well. No author can be sure about these requirements except those who only write textbooks for students in a familiar curriculum and who have continuous feedback from those students as well. Nevertheless, something like a master's degree in computer science is assumed, or an equivalent experience. Literacy of a similar level, and the humanistic interests of a responsible intellectual are also presupposed.

It may be surprising that no math is used although the topic is deeply related to mathematics. I hope that the reason for this is clear from what has been said above.

Is there anything new in this book? I doubt it; my statements reflect eternal questions. The experiences I have collected, whether of others or my own, are, I believe, similar to those of anybody who is working in this field. Nevertheless, equally true are the two statements from Ecclesiastes (the Book of The Preacher): "All the rivers run into the sea, yet the sea is not full; unto the place whither the rivers go, thither they go again." - 1:7. "The thing that has been, it is *that* which shall be; and which is done, is that which shall be done; and *there is* no new *thing* under the sun." - 1:9 (emphasis added).

1991

Foreword

After about fifteen years since my first book about computer epistemology was published, I decided to complete a review of further progress in computer science and of my own personal views and experience. I found shortly that the original book is still valid, nothing had to be corrected, but there was much to add, especially regarding the epistemic lessons and their background in mathematical basics.

Concerning these, an introductory chapter explains the epistemic relations of computer science and the information age. It emphasizes the role of computers in the transformation of communicational contents. Computers have emerged as the intermediate agent of most of our activities.

The second chapter is devoted to the fundamental role of algebra, the developmental origin of formal thinking, necessary for the formalization of any task.

The third chapter follows the line of this formalization by algebra and the fourth is devoted to all problems beyond logical formalization—the uncertainty issue.

The last chapter is a return to the epistemic lesson, to the constructive skepticism idea.

This essay does not claim to be a textbook, nor does it have the required precision of such a kind. This is the reason for several soft definitions, for the abbreviated explanations in the appendices, and for the relevant role and caricaturist style of the illustrations. The appendices are short references to necessary conceptual knowledge, specific information, and some definitions.

This kind of interpretation opens the pitfalls of reductionism into the abyss of trivialities. The essential ideas of science look to be obvious after a period of sedimentation and this further crystallization help the observers in getting a birds-eye view over rather wide disciplines. Newtonian mechanics and Maxwellian electrodynamics can be referred as examples.

This mental-learning process elevates simultaneously the gist of the subject and hides the real depth of the problem and of the related ways of thinking. This is the reason why I try to define the character of the work, and offer the reader an apology for the soft style.

The references to the literature suggest textbooks for those who would like to get more professional knowledge.

CHAPTER 1

Why Computer Epistemology?

1.1. Prologue: Why?

1.1.1. FIRST ANSWERS: OBVIOUS?

"Quidquid agis, prudenter agas et respice finem."
Whatever you do, do cautiously, and look to the end.

The practice of a critical view of all kind of activities is a useful activity in itself. Creating some professional procedures for critical views is also useful. This book puts an emphasis on the mathematical-computational instruments of our computer and information technology supported activities, and by this focuses on more general philosophical considerations.

The reasons for a review of the mathematical-computational arsenal are obvious, the philosophical detour is reasonable, due to the ubiquity of highly complex, computer and information controlled systems.

The application of all these ideas changes our worldview and the worldview changes the applications. Where, how, why, and why not, after all depend on our human relations and human attitudes, concerning especially the rapid development of technology.

The long, connected line of computational procedures has a different kind and quantity of treatment in the literature. Each task of this sequence is vulnerable due to failures or misuse of the applied methods, the problems of computational and human-understanding interfaces. The responsibility for these failures is often dubious, just due to the ever-increasing length and complexity of the conceptual and computational process.

The most comprehensive treatment of these avoidable and unavoidable problems can be found in the literature on computational tasks, programming, and applications in various different subjects. The theoretically deepest analysis of mathematical methods has the greatest past and a solid, fertile present. A weaker point of the whole is naturally the interface, the connection between the problem as a technological, social reality and their mathematical and computational representation. The same is valid in the non-computational human world, understanding different professional languages and different professional viewpoints.

The inserted mathematical and computer interface-representation can be even more dangerous. It lacks the direct feedback of dialogue and hides the problems in the more exact looking pseudo-objectivity of mathematics and computational technology. The first appearance of this phenomenon, much before computer technologies, was the realization of ambiguities in voting and in using statistics. The ambiguity of logic was an antique predecessor.

The analysis of inherent limitations and leakages can be, in their major part, summarized under the conceptual frame of epistemology, the analysis of understanding, meaning, processes of abstraction. The interface between the understood or hypothetical nature of a problem and its mathematical model representation is our challenging subject. It should evoke interest not only due its specific nature but also as being an important exercise in ways of thinking about our everyday computer-supported life.

After *Computer Epistemology* (Vámos, 1991), published nearly two decades ago, this discussion tries to highlight the novelties of the period. Speaking about novelties, I return once again to very ancient considerations. The contrast, as usual, verifies the valuable novelties on the market of ideas and methods.

I concentrate on our theoretical instruments and their implementations. Why should we deal with parts of the computer-supported methods and realizations that have firm theoretical bases, and are professionally best developed and proven in practice? Simply because, due to these merits, in their applications the theoretical bases raise less doubts, whether the choice of the theoretical instrument is locally correct.

This essay, as was clarified in the cited preface, tries to approach the problems in different ways. This reflects not only glances at the supposed readers but also how the author tries to understand and put together these broad, basically multidisciplinary subjects. That is the reason of the rather funny figures and cartoons that simplify the concepts and the sometimes longer appendices, with a few more details.

Illustrations of all these abstractions put more vivid light on the subject. In Appendices 1.1 and 1.2, both projects are sketched in a simplified way. These were developments and are working successfully as the result of long efforts in our Institute's groups. They required deep theoretical work, innovative approaches, applicable for broad classes of real life, practical, and complex tasks.

1.1.2. FURTHER GENERAL LESSONS

Examples crop up in many other settings. Scheduling a medical diagnostic center or working with other, partly serial, partly sequential resources, e.g., traffic control, social services and systems can be treated by analogous models. Automatic control, control based on sensory systems, organs and adjusting, compensating systems in cases of expected, and non-expected, stochastic disturbance situations: that is the general task of every dynamic, living, individually, and collectively behaving system. They can be found in every technology, biological creature, and society.

Multivariate control, of Appendix 1.1, based on several sensory effects, create a world of co-operation and hierarchy. Co-operation means weighting the individual inputs, according their temporal behavior, reliability, importance in the situation concerned, hierarchy according to the same considerations and filtering in cases of logical contradictions. The temporal, logical-hierarchical state of the system governs the commutativity and distributivity of the effects, their operational features individually and in groups. Let us think about the sophisticated, harmonically balanced operation of steering, braking, gas control of a long vehicle which faces a sudden curvature, a vehicle passing in the opposite direction, and all that on a slippery road. The automatic control of the system cannot pray or swear, it has to find the optimal or best possible coherent action.

The illustration is the outline of one of the most ambitious European vehicle control projects. The complexity is apprehensible by the application of more than a hundred processors applied in one car and the more than one hundred special company code (MB) as a computer language transformation of the sensory and control task, comprising five autonomous but coordinated systems within the single vehicle.

The control is supported by some kind of knowledge. This knowledge is hidden in the primitive control settings but can be a highly complex knowledge base on nonlinear dynamics, all kinds of road signals, a compendium of human experience, and simulation games. Logic and algebra of mathematical analysis are the fundamentals of modeling. All kinds of dynamic equilibria, disequilibria, changes of states, and material-energy forms have unique expressions in Lie-groups and Lie-algebras. That will be the subject of Chapter 2 and 3.

The scheduling in Appendix 1.2 is a typical logical construct; the handling of contradictions means the application of some conditionals; the individual operations means a rather complete description in languages that can lead to machine control programs. Considering the limits of logic, used as an instrument for reasoning, we design the correct reasoning, based on these scheduling programs and all similar tasks.

Limits of logic are defined also by the transformations applied by the programs. These transformations get material meaning in the manufacturing example. The material handling operations are represented by transformation programs of work piece geometries and material-phase, composition, and production technology. Transformation operations are basically algebraic operations in mathematics, with their strict rules, regarding permissible and not permissible transformations, due to the predetermined definitions of the components. The rules of commutativity direct the possibility of changing the order of operations applied—substitution of one operation or operator by another—like milling and drilling in several cases. In the rules of associativity—the permissible grouping of manufacturing actions—inversion may mean a melting reformation, though the definition of the unity state can be dubious. Similarly, the permissible and not permissible operations in any professional activity can and mostly should be attributed to certain logically well-defined object groups. That disciplinary clarity of ways of thinking is necessary for creating and executing programs influencing anything but cannot be comprised mentally in their overall complex, reused details.

The general scheme of scheduling a complex industrial process with co-operation of several different manufacturing workshops was a simplified result of a project in the several billion-dollar production chain. One part of the mathematical formulations is added as an illustration of the quoted translation mechanisms.

The scheduling problem, similarly to the control of different mechanisms and different aims, is burdened by different and changing strategies. The interests and the information bases of the participants are not the same, mostly contradictory and in most cases not even formulated in a clear way. A good example is the balance among expenses, safety of operation, and quality of service. The usual models of these strategies are reductive algorithms, and in spite of all the simplifications and vague hypotheses of people's behavior, the computational task runs out of reasonable limits.

All ways lead to uncertainty. Our primitive example excluded them but not the reality of demand, future markets, reliability of tools, materials, and primarily, people. Dealing with uncertainty is, of course, a delicate part of the quoted projects. Uncertainty has nearly mystically infinite faces, all those are linked to certain more standard models of experience and reasoning. Game theory, with applications of mathematical models for psychological attitudes and response types are a recent expanding armory for computer assisted consultation and decision support in model-driven considerations of scheduling production and market environments. These methods are more and more applied in argumentations about questions of global human coexistence and survival.

How to orient our responsibility-driven actions mediated by computers and other information technologies is the practical meaning of epistemology for engineering, medical practice, economist planning, and social orientation.

1.2. Knowledge about Knowledge

"All the wise men of antiquity," Roger Bacon wrote in the fourth book of his Opus Maius, "worked in mathematics so that they might know all things, as we have seen in some scholars of our own times, and as we have heard of in others who learned all knowledge through mathematics, which they knew well. For there have been some famous men, such as Robert, Bishop of Lincoln, and Brother Adam Marsh and many others, who have known how, by the power of mathematics, to unfold the causes of all things and to give a sufficient explanation of human and Divine phenomena. This is assured by the writings of these great men, for example by their works on the impression [of the elements], on the rainbow, on comets, on the generation of heat, on the investigation of the places of the world, on celestial things, and on other questions appertaining both to theology and to natural philosophy. And so it is obvious that mathematics is absolutely necessary, and useful, to the other sciences."

Quoted by A. C. Crombie (1994)

1.2.1. Epistemology: The Most Important Practical Instrument

Epistemology—knowledge about knowledge—is a critical tool for a very practical purpose. Epistemology, in its practical aspect, is an attitude and method for investigating the serviceable merits of any kind of knowledge. It is, in the modern sense, a capacity of knowledge engineering. The definition itself, being rather circular, tells upon the essentially intrinsic nature of our self and species characterization substance. Perception, learning, information, memory, meaning, awareness, wisdom, and some other synonyms are not only used for

Epistemology—knowledge about knowledge

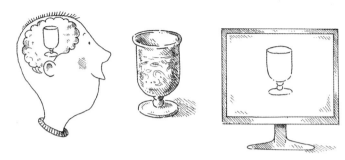

Reality and representations

circumscription–they all have vast philosophical and related professional literature for explanations and contradictory interpretations.

Treating knowledge about anything starts with the questions: *What is it about? Where does it come from? What can it be used for or what can be used from and by the knowledge for what? What can be used for the problem in question?* The question of how comes last: *How to apply, what are the constraints of application, how should the result be checked, treated in and for instruction, maintained monitored, and revised?*

1.2.2. PHILOSOPHY?

That is all inclusive! This is epistemology, in a decent formulation, a fundamental chapter of philosophy. From a purist and rationalist point of view: epistemology is philosophy itself. Ontology, the philosophy of Being, is related rather to beliefs, theology, metaphysics, i.e., everything beyond our practical reality.

The word, *ontology,* is now appropriated by computer specialists for the classical exercise of categorization and interpretation, like epistemology in the role of verbal interpretation and computer representation of knowledge. Different applications of the same words are rather usual, similarly to our case, it can reflect a trend for more elegant-looking denominations. The link, between the two ontology concepts, can be very distant, used only for cases referencing to our human existence.

All other disciplines, under the classic, ancient umbrella of philosophy, are disintegrated into and by the referenced sciences, mathematics, physics, biology, and, of course, social sciences, history, sociology, and law. *Ethics* and *esthetics* also have ontological origins. Their human aspects reappear as specifics and generalities of philosophical considerations. This relational coherence comes back with the treatment of a *constructive skepticism*. Psychology as ever, has been more a branch of humanities, it is an example of developing bridges between classic science and anthropological knowledge. Our knowledge-based man-machine world reopens the habitual human questions with every relevant application and at any time from new and more complex aspects.

Several sciences of this man-machine dichotomy are going to be recombined—e.g., linguistics, ethics, logic, psychology, history, economy, and many other disciplines. This recombination drives the interest of research and practice towards epistemic, knowledge-oriented philosophy. Our ancient desire to see and understand the world as a consistent whole, and especially consistent for our judgments, is a driving force of any kind, popular or highbrow, philosophizing.

Returning to our examples, the task of manufacturing depends on the changing values of the product, its raw material and fabrication economy, application qualities, esthetics, fashionable design and some features related to the ethics of environmental and working safety effects. The scheduling game runs in a scheme of limited information about the customer population, with some hypotheses about their purchase power, habits, sometimes about weather and other stochastic conditions. Sociology, anthropology, geography, a lot of human-related knowledge should be accumulated within problem solving.

The vehicle control design is not less sensitive to human ethical and esthetic relations, regarding the prospective drivers and human environments of the commuting regions.

On one hand, all these qualities of a system-design responsibility were required in earlier periods of engineering. Reading the classic work of *Vitruvius* (1960), we find the sophisticated humanistic-oriented origins of system design. The main difference, not to be emphasized enough, is now the necessary mathematical-programming model between the task and the system. The model is an art of molding knowledge into the program and that means a scientific conceptualization method in a strong sense of science, clarifying all details and connections that were intuitive capabilities of the earlier masters.

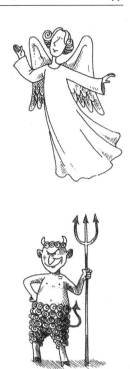

Beyond epistemology: metaphysics

This is the meaning of computer epistemology, a new, necessary development of an old branch of philosophy.

What remains beyond that epistemic ability, lies in the infinite ocean of metaphysics, lies beyond the coasts of science, until it is not conquered by epistemic means, like several early questions of cosmology or the determinism vs. free will debate. How we approach the necessary problems in a temporary and progressive way will be treated in the chapter about uncertainty and approximation methods.

Not arguing much about these basic and historical problems of philosophy, I would like emphasize only the fundamental relevance of epistemology. This argumentation can easily be caught by the same reasoning, similarly to the other disintegrations. How to use a certain method of uncertainty calculation is a question of the mathematical theory and nature of the application task, rather than a philosophical problem about uncertainty in general.

True, we can say from a pragmatic point of view. Epistemology is preferably an attitude and methodology for knowledge, representation, and by that, more a philosophy, before the real application. But in this role, it is a necessary, unavoidable step in application itself. We shall see how much consideration can be required for a decision, what kind of uncertainty is really the question, for example, if a problem of driving control is the uncertainty of weather conditions or of human psychology. Most of the necessary active control devices and even more the settings of their parameters depend on these circumstances, not to speak about the previous selection of the vehicle type and its accessories.

The same can be said about production scheduling. Looking at the simplified operation scheme, anybody can point a finger on the various uncertainty sensitivities and their very different temporal and statistical distribution nature.

The statement *true* is really dubious in all pragmatic details of complex problems. Design, especially in its problem-statement phase, is a decision process of necessary and not necessary looking circumstances, a highly relative and responsible task. The connection between these circumstances considering decisions and the selection of the most appropriate computational-modeling methods is the next, still epistemic, i.e. knowledge-based and philosophically based step—knowledge-based on the professional designer expertise, and philosophically-based on the views of the designer and the customers. Customers are the investors and the prospective users, relative are all facts and views about those, their epistemics.

The dubious meaning of the word *true* is the archetype of epistemology! After epochal great ancestors, we come back to the truth problem, renewed and sharpened by computer epistemology and information-technology practice.

In this book I am trying to demonstrate the above statement.

1.2.3. ... AND COMPUTER EPISTEMOLOGY?

Computer epistemology, in the scope of this book, is a very special chapter of the philosophy realm and especially of epistemology. The reason lies in the social role of computers and communication. Social

Communication in different ages

role means a totally novel intermediate stance between knowledge and its application, somehow similar to an interpreter between two people, and what is more, between two societies having different languages. Different languages mean not only the narrow sense of vocabularies and grammars but also the ways of thinking, references of different cultures to different stories, meanings, and affections.

Man started to operate with hands and soon (in a few hundred thousand or million years) with tools. Though using tools is a typical human trait, some intelligent animals share these beginnings. Tools developed to a high sophistication until the present, and their use was amplified by power generation. The operation of and on the objects remained in rather direct contact with the human operator via the tools. Instruction and control related to these operations was a normal linguistic task, though sometimes by using special terms and figures. Nevertheless, the direct contact and direct control remained within the frame of operation. This hundred thousand years old direct contact of man-to-man and man-to-execution of the task is now broken. The world of information connects actions, relations which are distant physically and in temporal relation, but on the other hand, by interposing communication lines and computers, information creates a new alienation, a new feeling of losing direct contact, insight, and responsibility.

The conscious knowledge view and the view on knowledge in that broken contact—how we revise our earlier knowledge and how we have to use our previous and newly required knowledge—*is the meaning of computer epistemology.*

1.2.4. ALIENATION AND SEPARATION OF THE REPRESENTATION

Teleoperation itself is a not-so-esoteric picture of the novelty. The main issue is the alienation and separation of the representation. The ancestor of that phenomenon is the separation of *writing* and *reading* of a text, separated in time and culture, but that was not a general practice for everyday life. A recipe is also a certain teleoperator, a written command. This early sophistication required people with special linguistic knowledge and cultural background, and the difference in interpretation was in some respects accepted, though it could have tragic outcomes in the history of malevolence, obscurantism, and dogmatic beliefs.

The technological separation of activities

The primary distance between reality and abstracted knowledge had distanced relations between the two. Weak feedbacks and strong psychological effects of the superior interpretations were the consequences. These interpretations had a much less epistemic nature and a much more ontological message. Steering a vehicle or scheduling a certain production involves much more direct feedback to the reality than myths about the origins of rulers or forecasts about the future.

The technological separation of activities brought about different professional methods, and description-modeling languages. The present situation characterized by the interposition of computers, as the cases in modern numerical control, surgical teleoperation, flight control or coordinating activities of people, created the need for some unifications in the modeling, computer applicable representations and methods.

Interfacing different representations is, first of all, a methodological problem and that is the essence of treating computer epistemology as a knowledge philosophy of our Information Age. The problem is wide, due to the generality of application in all kinds of operations among us and related to the external world. Most of the traditional jobs and everyday activities changed, from being results of direct contact and powered by human force, to operating computers. That new reality is mostly hidden in one or the other machine.

What happens in between depends highly on the application and performance of these hidden knowledge transformers, though the simplest innocent user should have a view, if not a knowledge, on what is going on, what can be expected.

If this is not the case, and what is usually the factual situation more than the appropriate insight, the chief designer on the one end, or the application manager on the other end should have the whole responsibility for all unknown users and intermediate people and actions. The responsibility is incorporated in the knowledge of all respects, enumerated in the previous chapter.

Knowledge, never before so complex and demanding, due to the mass and remote application, is a postulate for computer epistemology.

1.2.5. THE EPISTEMIC FEEDBACK LOOP

The scheme is meant to explain the general epistemic process and its conceptual world. It reflects the typical present course of research for a new frame of knowledge. The process starts with observation of the phenomena, gathering all kinds of possibly related preliminaries, data, hypothetical analogies, and coherence. The conclusion is a new, or reaffirmed, extended theory. Most important are the *feedbacks* in each procedural step, and finally, regarding the phenomenon, the object–the real problem itself. Each step should incorporate its experience and theory-based quality check, rules of experimentation- environment, number and frequency of repetition, transparency and accessibility of the procedures. These rules of the procedures are subjects of similar research conducts. The characteristics of statistics, putting on record the data of the physical, chemical, and other types of environmental, temporal constraints are parts of these professional rules of research.

The reader can easily substitute the referential procedural items of the examples or of other professional activities into the general scheme, giving a more intelligible representation of required checks in following responsibilities of complex operations. The scheme can have other ways of binding activities, e.g., separating the experimental, measuring phase from the first steps of data, information processing. The essential quality is the feedback necessity and the consequential design.

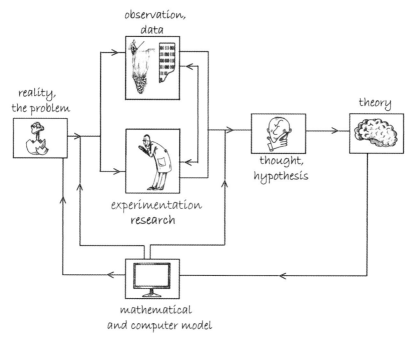

observation, data

reality, the problem

theory

thought, hypothesis

experimentation research

mathematical and computer model

The epistemic feedback loop

The procedures of current, science-based knowledge acquisition are the security means of authentic knowledge against charlatanry and deception, any kind of pseudoscience. This problem returns several times in the discussion and as an even more relevant issue in everyday practice. The standpoint of the constructive skepticism cannot permit any final truth, not even for any up-to-date science, and equally cannot avoid the application of proven practical methods based on consolidated scientific knowledge. This balanced wisdom is the essence of our persistence of epistemic considerations, our ethical stance in science and our responsibility to openness and knowledge.

1.2.6. Evolutionary Process of Representation

All these procedures went through their own evolutionary process, and that is the reason why the adjective *current* is used, but the essential feature of having feedbacks had to be present from the very

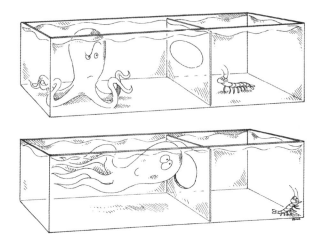

The learner and recognizer octopus

beginning. The fundamental feedback scheme characterizes our essential concepts: *representation* and *model*.

Phenomena reach the observer via sensory inputs of the sensory organs. For the longest time of evolution these are the direct sensory inputs of biology, the biochemical transformations of the signals available from the vitally important substances, e.g., food, inimical phenomena, obstacles, shelters, reproduction. The most primitive living creatures—ancestors of plants and animals—worked on these schemes. That is the origin of information, information received by the mentioned transformations activated the movement, phenomena of life. The mechanism is the primitive form of representation.

Representation in this primitive form is the start of *adaptivity* and *learning*, observed also in sea slugs (Aplysia), the experimental primitive mollusks of Eric Kandel (1956, 1970), the Nobel-prized pioneer of neural response research. John Y. Young (1956) observed the amazing learning capabilities of the octopus, on the *reachability* of its favorite lobsters.

The octopus, after some learning experiments, could distinguish a circle from an ellipse. In this experiment the circle was the signal of free access on a glass wall, the second of the closed state. These creatures have no central neural system compared to more developed creatures; one hundred million years of evolution led to the impressive knowledge acquisition, memory storage, and representation abilities of animals of higher intelligence.

Why do I dwell so long on the origins of the epistemic loop? This serves a more objective view of concepts surrounded later by some vague sophistication—by truth-certainty argumentations of some strong AI prophets, on the one hand, and metaphysical uncertainty ideas on the other.

Some AI-robotics people try to deduce all human and human-like actions to the available and short term predictable sensory pattern-recognition, signal-unification, decision, and motion-control schemes.

Thinkers, inclined more toward metaphysics, refer to the infinite variety of human responses, the utmost delicate representations of sentiments, art's immeasurable depths, to the non-repeatable nature of individuals. The estimated hundred million years of evolution stands against the rational sophistication of up-to-date technology. The endlessly final conclusion is left to the end of this book.

The transformation processes of representations developed along roads of objective necessities and through the means of natural biological propagation. This dual evolution guarantees the fantastic ampleness of reality, anchored in our mind and epistemic instrumentation—though bearing in mind its limitations—due to the same

The robot and the creative mind

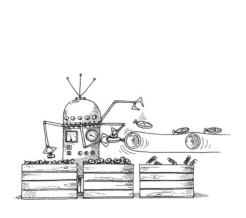

biological processes. In both the obvious and the hidden perceptive structures, learning abilities of our mind are evolutionary imprints of evolutionary encounters with reality, exercised infinite times during the last one hundred million years. This is our precious heritage for creative survival and simultaneously our heavy burden as a mechanism of obsolete responses. The new situation of direct feedback via indirectly acting communication and processing channels is our current challenge.

1.2.7. The Model: Practical and Relativistic Representation for Computer Understanding

Model in our discourse is a human development of representation. The representation phenomenon is present in all, more or less, intelligent animals, too, but the ability of a *secondary representation*–the representation of the brain representation by words–is definitely human. It can be associated with the verbal facility. In this sense, the

Real object, model, manufacturing, program file

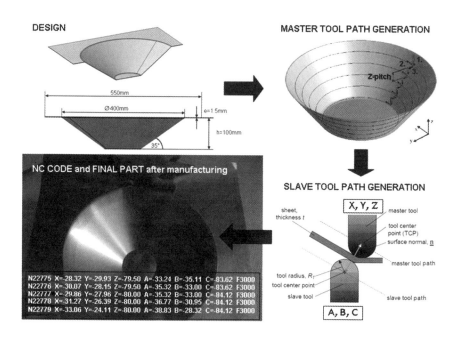

model is a linguistic version of representation, developed from the realistic-mystic descriptions of environmental impressions into sophisticated, structured definitions, and further, the circumscriptions of selected and related phenomena.

The concept of the model has two special meanings for us. The first is related to the mode of description, and that is the extension of *linguistic representation* towards a machine-understandable formulation via the conceptual instruments of philosophy, logic, and linguistics. A special role is instrumental by the professional linguistics of the disciplinary frame, to be represented. This part of representation procedure is, usually, identified with the concept of ontology, used in the computer technology vernacular.

The next step towards a computer model is the mathematical formulation of the linguistic model and based on that, it is the program itself. All these steps are strongly linguistic procedures; the program is *the* machine-understandable language.

The second meaning has a special epistemic relevance: *the model is a representation and not the reality to be described*. It is a practical reduction and a relativistic picture. Both relativistic features are main subjects.

1.2.8. MODELS SUGGEST HYPOTHESES AND THEORIES

Representations interact, similarly to representations of real life interactions. Representations of persons, actors interact with representations of actions, objects, other actors representing ownerships, objectives, and other relations. These representation interactions are reflected in the syntactic structures of the languages, sentences, paragraphs and more detailed *communications*. This is the essential meaning of languages: instruments of communication, in the current subject: man-machine and vice versa. Several laboratory and more advanced robotics and animation systems recognize basic expressions of emotional states and emulate expressions of hypothetical responses. These interactions are mostly obvious facts, like in our figure about consuming some food, and representation in the mind on the other end of the communication line.

A *hypothesis* is generated by all these interactions and their consequences, e.g., feeling satisfied, enjoyment, or nausea. The next

Communication and associated sceneries

communication can be feedback on the hypotheses. The hypotheses are anchored into the *theories* of gastronomy, medical gastroenterology and biochemical metastasis. These theories should be continuously revised, and this fact and necessity are expressed, and then fed back by our changing taste, furthermore, the changing medical instructions, like those about the usefulness and dangers of butter and margarine, or of egg-white and yolk.

The epistemic lesson is to drink a good glass of cabernet sauvignon and start with the history of our subject, as the latest epoch of the evolutionary epistemic process, leading in a relatively direct and short way to computer epistemics!

1.3. Did It Start with the Greeks?

Dear Sir,

The development of Western Science has been based on two great achievements, the invention of the formal logical system (in Euclidean geometry) by the Greek philosophers, and the discovery of the possibility of finding out causal relationships by systematic experiment (Renaissance). In my opinion one need not be astonished that the Chinese sages have not made these steps. The astonishing thing is that these discoveries were made at all.

Sincerely yours,
A. Einstein,
Quoted and first published by D.J. de Solla Price (Price, 1961)

1.3.1. Yes!

The answer is an uncertain yes. Looking back to the partly known Egyptian and Mesopotamian origins, we find lots of elementary algebraic findings, generalizations, and important elements of linguistics inherited from Persian and Indian sources. I return to them in the discussion of derivate subjects. Analysis of the Chinese tradition is beyond my capacity. A devoted and better learned philosopher of science history could probably analyze these evolutionary processes and explain the similarities and differences of further cultural developments. *From the point of view of current information science and, therefore of this book, the continuations of Greek philosophy are the massively determining facts.*

The main difference is deeply epistemic and that is the reason why that feature is emphasized within these preliminaries. All previous results, what we are able to collect from the scarce archeological remains, were clearly phenomenological observations. Counting, measurement, recording, everything related to the practical tasks of construction, preservation, distribution of goods, and forecasts of meteorological conditions—all these belong to phenomenology. Each is important for food production and for social, power-oriented interests, much like how geography is important for trade and warfare.

Phenomenological observations were connected to the developing human interest in explanations of the world order, but these ways of thinking were a rather detached activity, on the lines of the mystic origins of metaphysics and theology. It was detached in ways of thinking and not in persons and social roles. The detachment of the two intelligent activities was strengthened by the social systems of the regions. Ancient Greece started to represent a different scheme of development by her distributed societies, by traveling and trading among people of different social orders, and by different world explanations.

The Greeks started the professional activity of *thinking about thinking*, about the epistemic elaboration of phenomena. They started the critical review of knowledge which can be considered the beginning of science in our sense. That was the origin of epistemology, i.e. the centuries long discourse about different interpretations of phenomenologically observed knowledge.

The discourse has no ends and most probably will never have one, at least until science works on observations and creates new interpretations and grand theories.

1.3.2. New Interpretations are Derived from New Observation Instruments

The great epistemic revolutions are mainly results of new instrumentations and new observation methods. The ancient world was restricted to the observations of the natural sensory organs and that is the reason for their limitations, and for the very practical, proven use of knowledge received by that limited possibility. The preserved inheritance and conservatism of that knowledge during the Middle Ages had, beyond other social-historical reasons, its roots in those observational limitations. The real revolution started by the two related optical instruments, the microscope and the telescope, a new look at the micro- and the mega-world opening in the Renaissance and the Age of Reason.

These shallow, bird's-eye-view statements about many hundred years of sometimes slowly progressing and many times contradictory, wobbling processes can be criticized by numerous counterexamples. One of them could be the renaissance persistence in antique science, as a renewed attitude after some more liberal ideas of the late Middle Ages. These pre-renaissance results were typically epistemic-related, of course, from another point of view, as will be discussed later in problems relating to logic.

Nevertheless, all major evolutions in the ways of thinking are bound to the possibilities of observation. This cannot be denied in relation to science. The acknowledgement of new facts is the major vehicle towards further steps in creating more adequate and efficient world models. The progressive development of these general

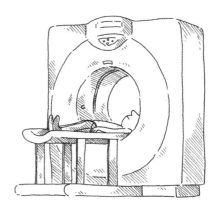

Observation in the past and today

models generate extensive applications, as the problem solving of celestial mechanics stimulated more practical advances in the models of motion. The meaning of adequacy and efficiency is expressed by these kinds of extensions and they are, by that effect, the filters of vague speculations. These steps are well measured in discoveries of new scales and new dimensions not previously observable.

The next revolution, partly continuing to our age, is also bound to the development of observational instrumentation of modern physics and chemistry, influencing the observational possibilities of biology, too. For anybody even superficially familiar with these results, there is no need to enumerate those.

1.3.3. The Observational and Epistemic Novelty of Computer Technology

Computer technology created three essential observational novelties. The first is the influence on the *development of instrumentation*. Computer tomography, in its ever extending forms of using different physical methods, is only the most obvious appearance of all kinds of observational tools driven by and composed of electronic, information-technology methods.

Computer-assisted technologies prepared the advent, in their direct and indirect consequences, of micro-analytical and observational instruments of molecular, atomic, and subatomic phenomena. All new perspectives of genetics, cosmology, nanotechnology, and medical practice are, more or less, results of this technology and its influence, its supreme ubiquity.

The second novelty is *data processing*. For the first time in history science could manage the immense quantity of data and information acquired through observation. Science could also receive the immense amount of data necessary for the elaboration of mass phenomena. The latter possibility is strongly related to new technology emphasized above. Data processing and data mining create new international virtual laboratories where distributed groups of scientists collect observational data and work on evaluation and interpretation of those never before available factual bases.

After the input and processing revolution, the third novelty is the new nature of output. In most production tasks and in a great number of other critical applications—e.g., flight control—the output is a direct control program for an executing machine (a robot, for example), a machine tool, a vital valve in a chemical plant, or in a life-supporting apparatus during surgery.

In this way, for the first time in history, results of science interact in a direct manner with everyday and critical moments in life. For the first time, knowledge was responsible for action. Critical, epistemic knowledge is now a vital requirement.

1.3.4 How Deep? And Depth, What Does it Mean?

Should a programmer of a given task submerge into the development of meanings, starting from the beginnings of grammatical-semantic theories? Should he or she be simultaneously an expert of the subject to be programmed, e.g., the kinematics related to robots? What is this kind of philosophical mathematical essay for the practitioner of computer technology?

My starting point is the volatility of programming languages, their claims for generality on the one hand and their detailed practical instruments for representation in singular programming tricks, flexible interfaces, any kinds of savings, and extending special services, on the other.

To some extent, in order to be versatile in professional life, anybody on any level may receive relevant help by a certain higher, more stable level of knowledge that generates individual solutions. The conceptual levels of thinking and communication were developed by the same need for communication and understanding economy. The conceptual level contains, in a direct or hidden way, its critical elements by the wrapping of similarities, associations, and, by those, a certain check with issues experienced and examined earlier. The concept by its associative power provides reference for understanding not only the item concerned but its place within the knowledge realm, i.e., references of validity to other applications.

This was the story of linguistic evolution. Individual names of objects and actions received conceptual hulls and this started the critical epistemic considerations about the strength and weaknesses of the conceptual levels, first about the dangers and usefulness of some animals. Erroneous classification, due to misconceptions, can be a bone of contention among specialists. The practicality and epistemic problem of generalization puts light on an essential motivation of this book.

Classifying and typifying individual knowledge-pieces is a long-applied and powerful device for science. Misclassification can be stimulating if it suggests analogies or doesn't fit new knowledge, otherwise it is harmful; it is at its worst when used for ethnical prejudices. The rather old problem of languages and vernaculars is relevant for explanation of historical processes, migrations, understanding ancient texts, and changes in phonological characteristics. The same can be disastrous in the role of political manipulations.

Knowledge, by its abstraction levels, creates a certain hierarchy, the practice of elementary arithmetic operations and the esoteric, abstract, modern algebra are instructive examples. Especially in technology and computer technology this is not a singular case, the width of application knowledge exceeds the ability and necessity of all widths and depths.

The knowledge of individually not known evolves into a requirement as important as the knowledge detail itself. The *knowledge-society* necessitates the knowledge of others and limitations of ours, e.g., persons, institutions, and disciplines. In a common saying: *you have to know somebody, who knows somebody*. We may also say that this kind of knowledge of the width and depth of *society knowledge* is the essential reference of computer epistemology. Maybe, it is computer epistemology itself.

1.3.5. Our Conceptual World is Mathematics

We include into mathematics the chapters of philosophy and linguistics that were or were tried to be treated separately, e.g., logic. Chapter 3 will give more details on the reasons and further problems of logic dichotomy. For communication and computation, and for any practical use in the information age, the representation means the level of formulation that can be expressed by the instruments of mathematics. *Programming is not more and not less than a special linguistic translation of mathematical formulae.*

This important statement is criticized by ambitious software experts. The discussion is a good example of the meaning-generalization and specification mentioned above. Software engineering really developed into special skills, viewpoints, concepts, and methods. Software development and scientific methods of software engineering are now new emerging disciplines.

Conversely, any kind of scientifically firm statement about programs and about metalevels of programming should be formulated in an exact way, understandable by automaton. This was the great dream of Leibniz and achievement partly of Babbage and partly of Frege and the final ambition of those in AI. The meaning of this ambition, from my point of view, is the elevation of computer and specifically programming science to the rigor-requirement level of mathematics. Similarly to mathematics, this remark doesn't belittle the role of intuition in research heuristics but refers to the formularization requirements of software knowledge.

The lesson is here is that a mandatory level of mathematical erudition is required. By mandatory I mean the level of mathematical knowledge matched to the level of programming status hierarchy. This book is an attempt to give some indication toward this knowledge-matching exercise: an experiment in looking *at the practical meaning of depths.*

1.4. An Important Addendum about the Non-Formalized Human Issue

"Nil homini certum est: Nothing is certain for man"
Ovid, Tristia 5.5.27

1.4.1 ISSUES BEYOND...

I wrote in the previous subsection: *For communication and computation, and for any practical use in the information age, the representation means a level of formalization that can be expressed by the instruments of mathematics.* This sentence should also be an admonition to the issues that cannot be formalized in an abstract-pragmatic way, not at present and maybe never. These are the most important real ontological issues of human life and human relations. The strength and weakness of formalizations currently indicate the separations and interfaces of mankind from and to its creation, the mechanized service. A good example is e-government practice in which a thorough analysis separates tasks that can be executed in an automatic, rule-based way, e.g., issuing a certificate on the basis of available data, and those requiring human judgment, based on individual consideration and personal responsibility.

1.4.2 FURTHER STRUCTURE

The introduction tried to establish an agreement between the author and the reader about the problem statement and its relevance. (The author had to be convinced first—a skeptical person should have doubts about his/her devotions.) The last statement was about the role of mathematics in modeling and programming as being the original node of epistemic-critical investigation. Further steps of programming and application-oriented knowledge representation are more specific, related to programming technology and the fields of applications. The latter raise more obvious questions and that is the reason why they are much more widely treated in the literature and in everyday practice. In the past half century, during my professional career and in the activities of my research fellows, we encountered and had to solve many similar issues: control of power-plants and systems, governance organizations, large-scale projects in production and traffic control, and communication networks among others.

All problems involved hints to the partly hidden conceptual world of applied mathematics, and treatment of application tasks provoked interest for their general lessons. This book is a summary. Not as ambitious as our medieval ancestors compiling their theological, philosophical, logical ideas under the title of *Summa*. The review concentrates on some mathematical-epistemics which are considered to be the roots of our modeling world. The introductory chapter tried to explain their highly practical, vital importance. Subsequently, the further text will be treated according to the formal-structural essence of the mathematical background.

The original concepts stem from algebra, being in the specific role of *mater studiorum,* the mother of learning–learning structural abstractions from counting to the highest abstracted formalism.

The algebra- and philosophy-originated skeleton of program formulation is logic, the subject of the next chapter. What cannot be expressed by usual formulae of logic is the unlimited realm of uncertainty with the approximation methods that can be matched to the model of the problem to be treated.

The oft quoted sentence No. 7 in Wittgenstein's *Tractatus* (1922): "Whereof one cannot speak, thereof one must be silent," was softened by Wittgenstein himself. In our formulation: *what cannot be expressed by present means of representations and modeling should be circumvented, approximated, put partially or completely within some borders of knowledge–as far as possible.*

This is a renewed endeavor, after Galileo, for measuring everything measurable and making measurable everything possible. This kind of possibility search is another meaning of computer epistemology, the subject of Chapters 4 and 5.

CHAPTER 2

Algebra: The Discipline from the Simplest to the Most General

2.1. Introduction to the Game of Life and Thinking

Wie Alles sich zum Ganzen webt,
Eins in dem Andern wirkt und lebt!
....

Welch Schauspiel! aber ach! ein Schauspiel nur!
Wo faß ich dich, unendliche Natur?

(How all things live and work, and ever blending,
Weave one vast whole from Being's ample range!
....

A wondrous show! but ah! a show alone!
Where shall I grasp thee, infinite nature, where?)

Johann Wolfgang von Goethe, Faust[1]

2.1.1. GAME OF LIFE: THE SIMPLEST START?

Let us start with a thought-experiment. That is a common way of thinking about how to construct complex objects: define, or assume, or imagine a small set of basic components and a similarly small set of fundamental rules for combining of them. From the very start of computing history, games were designed in this way, following the great traditions of chess and similar amusing constructions. The *Game of Life*, first published in 1970 by John Conway, a British mathematician, stimulated by the ideas of *John von Neumann,* applies these obvious principles, and this was followed by a huge family of further developments. For a bit more detailed text and with a small

---

[1] The Goethe translations were mixed from George Madison Priest (1932) and the recent Gutenberg project texts. Neither can reflect the qualities of the original, not in a modest level.

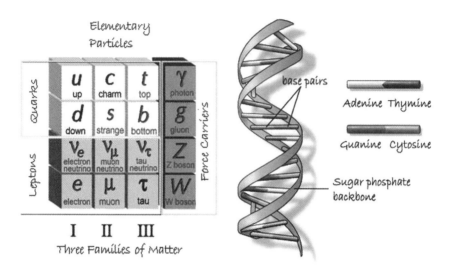

Elementary components of the universal game

insight into the relation of these game and machine prototypes, see Appendix 2.1.

This is what Science does generally: particle physics and theories of cosmology; chemistry starting with the concept of elements; biology and evolutionary theories. This characterizes the route, how science dug deeper and deeper toward the particles of the standard model of physics and biology, and toward the elementary codes of genetics–chemical compounds of the living creatures' bodies. The parallel effort was the search for combination rules of these primitives and all of their further combinations until the dimensions and changes of the Universe or the coexistence features of human masses.

The great route from elementary particles to the human brain and further is far from being reproduced, though more has been discovered in the past one hundred fifty years about these mechanisms than ever before. No evidence is available for the final success and none for the final failure. The partly successful and highly practical methodology of scientific thinking is remarkably modeled by the constructive production methods of algebra, and these constructive production methods are, in direct and indirect ways, working computational models in everyday problem solving.

2.1.2. GAME OF EPISTEMIC DEVELOPMENT: TANGIBLE OBJECTS...

Ways of human thinking and ways of the dynamics of Nature are similar, and not by chance. The ways of our brain and thinking development are the imprints of our experience, related originally to tangible objects. We meet the fundamentals of epistemology: the relation between reality and the represented, mirrored picture in our thinking. This general idea was outlined in the introduction. Now we go further with the analysis of the bases in mathematical modeling.

Let us follow that line with the way of thinking itself. That is the essential path from the point of view of computer representation. What can we represent and not represent in our computers? Here, *tangible* means a dramatically expanding world of directly and indirectly tangible objects by all kinds of sensory devices. Linguistically, these are represented mostly by nouns. We represent their relations by further linguistic instruments—further nouns, verbs, adjectives. These additions are the concepts of object entities, operations on objects and their concepts. The operations form the interactions of objects—their dynamics—quite similarly to the above pattern of

The primitive grammar

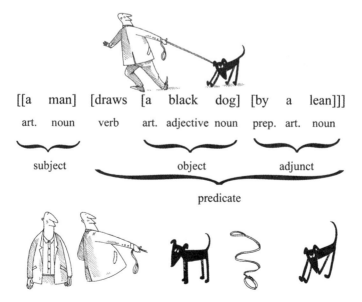

creative thought, which involve the means of *grammar* for representation of more complex interactions of objects.

The evolutionary history of language can be now tracked by linguistic observations of primitive, insulated tribes and prior to that on linguistic perception of primates. A next scientific-epistemic step is the discourse on imprinting this communication-evolution into the biological evolution of the brain. The evolution of language represents the evolution of ways of thinking, similar to the role of our eyes being a reflective organic part of the brain, much more in this essential function and organization than a window outside of the skull. The relation of language and perceptive functions of the brain is the gist of the Chomskyan linguistic theory. According to Chomsky (1957), and reinforced now by many new results of brain-research biology, some structural linguistic abilities are present in the evolutionary heritage of the whole human race.

This primitive grammar illustrates the evolutionary development of the linguistic and mental root of conceptual thinking.

2.1.3. And Further Toward Structures of Objects...

According to a post-Chomskyan evolutionary theory, an early development in grammar happened a few ten thousand years ago with a mutation of the gene mostly responsible for speech (a version of FOXP gene). One of our ingenious ancestors invented the technology of weaving threads from elementary plant fibers and, as a great addition to the technique of making knots, this technology was used for further application in fishing and vestment. The distribution of work within the tribe was supported by the communication of the technology, and this required a little bit more than juxtaposition of different sounds and words. A structure of items in the operations, to think about, memorize, and teach needed and created the first grammar. Till now, no original documentation was found about the discovery but the logic is attractive. *Si non è vero è ben trovato*—if that is not true, is well conceived, (Uriagereka, 2005).

The next step to the bottom, that we would like to touch upon, is more related to the early origins of computation. Writing was, after verbal communication, the next step in intellectual evolution and abstracted representation.

The knot and the discovery of the universal grammar?

With the evolutionary bifurcation of writing composed of ideograms and shorthand symbols, a new representation of objects and their relations should have started to develop about six millennia ago or possibly earlier. The invention of the alphabet, composing the written words from individual characters, is usually attributed to the Phoenicians. Nevertheless, this development was a long historical process, as well, reaching its nearly present level with the Greeks. Although the characters were to represent individual sounds, the development created a next step of representation-abstraction (literally: *draw away*) of ways of thinking, another higher step of representation, an expression of object-relations.

This is the deep meaning of the representation-bifurcation. In one dominant culture, the Western Civilization, thinking and communication is built in a hierarchy of representation abstractions, with individual sound-originated characters—words composed by characters and grammars giving relational meaning to the message. In the other, no less fertile civilization, the ideogram development worked in the direction of pattern-oriented, associative thinking. It remained a powerful quality of the Far East, still operating as symbolic representation, and further towards rule-based abstractions. Skill in discrimination, recognition, and reproduction of fine patterns is not only a special art of Far Eastern calligraphy but a prolonged value in modern precision technologies.

These hypotheses are not yet proved in a firm way, and require further research in psychology and brain representations though the cultural evidence suggest them.

2.1.4. ... Interactions, Transformations...

The outlined instrument of the construction-model, now applied to representation methods, is the set of rules for combination of the objects–procedures for creating something new from the interaction of objects. The representation of the interactions, i.e., the systems of rules, may have a similar analogical hierarchical formation. It joined the system hierarchy of the objects naturally. The system of rules starts to be inevitable in a dynamic world where it is impossible to neglect the transformation of the objects, the returning features of construction-transformation processes.

The process may be followed by the surprising richness of ancient mathematical examples for solving individual problems of geometry (in the literal sense of measuring the land); in construction of three dimensional objects, e.g., houses, pyramids, and arithmetic for calendars, distribution of goods and similar, related problems. The emergence of rules is also impressive, starting with a lot of rather developed calculation algorithms in Mesopotamia, Egypt, and the East.

Simplest rules, simple execution algorithms

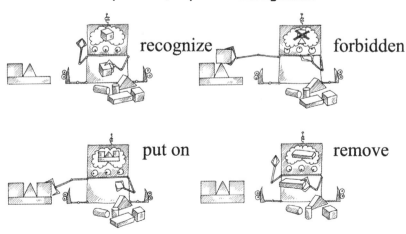

2.1.5. ... ALL SYMBOLIC

The other, even more determinant and remarkable bifurcation of the two leading civilizations started with the Renaissance, Reformation, and Age of Reason, a successive liberation from hard, consolidated social-political structures and associated, canonized conceptual systems. This development was manifested in the wealth of nations, in ways of thinking. All was in close connection with the emerging requirements of commerce, navigation, and new attitudes in the inquiry about the phenomena of nature. The new world demanded more advanced, more generally applicable, computable representations, the advancement of mathematics, specified in the theories of interaction, and dynamics and their necessary notations. The revolution of mathematical-logical notations, writing rules in formulae, started at the beginning of the 14th century and continued to follow closely the advances of calculus.

In Appendix 2.2 a short review demonstrates the evolutionary environment and developmental process of mathematical notation. Long ways of thinking and practice pave the avenue of representation-abstraction toward the mathematical bases of current programming techniques.

It should be emphasized that the progress of notation is essentially connected to the clarification of the conceptual content. The discussion of Newton and Leibniz demonstrate the relevance of appropriate notation from the point of view of additivity. Leibniz (1768, 1997), suggested the notation *d* for differential calculus, an operator applied still now, with the notion of embedded rules $d(x + y) = d\,x + d\,y$ and $d(x\,y) = x\,d\,y + y\,d\,x$ and illustrated his calculus with some examples, especially for geometric problems, in a rather modern sense. Another reference to conceptual depth: the addition is the origin of all further abstracted algebraic operations. Think about the operations on the Turing machine, which can do all these operations, of course, in a rather clumsy way! Notation developed with advancement from phenomenology to scientific structures of coherence, generalization, and application.

These remarks don't really refer to the priority quarrel of these two geniuses of scientific history. It indicates more the strong interest of Leibniz in mechanization of calculations, and on the other side Newton's in physics with the *flux* interpretations of infinitesimal calculus.

The 19th century development of notation and logic will be discussed more in detail in Chapter 3. The computer revolution followed in a direct instrumental way, with modern logic, computer languages, and notation. It is worth mentioning that some popular typesetting systems (e.g. T_EX) partly return to verbal definitions of the notational symbolism unifying the benefits of the braid of thinking development. The wording *braid* is a humble reference to the pioneering work of Hofstadter's *Gödel, Escher, Bach* (Hofstadter, 1979).

2.1.6. THE STORY OF THE INSTRUMENTS FOR REPRESENTING THE WORLD

I do not think it is possible to understand modern mathematics without at least having an overall idea of its history.

Dieudonné (1987)

The history of algebra is well documented in several textbooks. The beginnings in different cultures, especially the preferences developed through different heritages receive an impressive spectrum of views. (Shafarevich, 1997; van der Waerden, 1930–31).

Our short story in Appendix 2.3 presents the ideas of epistemic development from a rather narrow perspective of computer science. This story illustrates the ways of thinking more via the theoretical fundamentals and less via the brilliant progress of complex computer systems. The latter has excellent and nearly daily fresh literature, with their Turing-Neumann originated philosophies. (Penrose, 1989; Goldstine, 1972; Zemanek, 1991; IEEE Annals of the History of Computing.)

The two developments, of theoretical, logical fundamentals and advanced computer technology, are present mostly in the evolution of software, and can be somewhat discovered like an analogy of the developmental layers of the brain. The same or similar proteins and organisms support digestion in some primitive creatures, in the human gastroenterological system, and stimulate mental functions in the brain. The very early instruction and data structure ideas can be discovered with new contexts, advanced realizations in the current highly complex multiprocessor computing-systems.

The evolution of modern algebra is, in this mirror, the story of the construction from basic abstracted components–creating their hierarchy and establishing rules for combination and transformation of these objects into new, more general ones, towards the representation of new world models, first of all in physics. The story includes the developmental merger and separation of logic and algebra, manifested now in computer development.

That resistant and deeply working narrow origin and their combinations, immense in multitude though limited, represent our abilities and limitations, those of the computers and of the human beings as well. The number of possible combinations grows fast to a practically non-computable multitude. The complexity of simple, junior checkerboard games, of chess, and of any possible larger board game, e.g. go, are good examples of this growth in problem solving tasks. Our example for large scale production scheduling or the complexity of biological systems, human body, and behavior are the phenomena of everyday practice.

The emergence of non-computability can be experienced at the domino-tiling problem. Here one has to decide if the plane can be covered by a few types of dominos given as input. For the adjacency of tiles, the usual rules of a domino game apply.

In this course we can follow the Cantorian way of emerging cardinalities in infinity. Cardinality is the number describing the size of sets with the same number of elements. The set of natural numbers is infinite, but countable. The set of complex numbers is also infinite but their number of elements is much higher. The algorithmic process of complex problems follows the same track, requiring finite, countable, infinite but countable, and higher orders of the computational steps' multitude.

A highly relevant and wide open problem is the NP-P problem, encountered in our scheduling task. NP is a large class of algorithmic problems which amazingly includes many practical questions. Do we have efficient (polynomial time) algorithms for them? This is an open question, and the conjectured answer is *No*. The requirement of *polynomial time* is a meaningful abstraction of the *practical*. A polynomial can be of a large degree, hence a polynomial time algorithm can have very large time and memory requirement. The point is, however, that NP-hard problems appear to have even higher complexity, existing outside of this realm.

How computer science tries to overcome these issues will be the subject of the last chapters and related appendices.

I hope that the reader does not run out of patience at these lengthy, somehow nostalgic considerations; the purpose is a guidance into a very practical, though abstract-looking, thought process of putting ideas together, resulting in new ones, possibly mastering the ways to novelties. The last example—game-theoretical models for human responses in critical conflicts of economy and politics, honored with Nobel Prizes after their partial success in real life situations—can be proof of the practicality of our considerations.

The epistemic drive of thinking endows with constructive reduction and freedom as well.

2.2. Algebra, The Ladder from Counting to Coordinatizating the Universe

So, naturalists observe, a flea
Hath smaller flies that on him
prey;
And these hath smaller flies to
bite 'em,
And so proceed ad infinitum

Jonathan Swift, On Poetry, 337
or re-coordinated by a
mathematician:

Great flies have little flies
upon their backs to bite 'em
And little flies have lesser flies,
and so ad infinitum.
And the great flies themselves, in
turn have greater flies to go on;
While these again have greater
still, and greater still so on
Augustus de Morgan, *A Budget*
of Paradoxes, p. 377

2.2.1. Under the Umbrella...

Our concepts and conceptual instruments, used in computation and representation of the world by computational instruments, are born and developed under the umbrella of algebra. Other formulations of the rich branching structure of mathematics applied for modeling and computation permits other possible formulations about the origins, though this evocation of algebra looks to be, for the epistemic view, the most adequate and the most comprehensive disciplinary line. The way of our thinking, the evolutionary view suggests the approach. The historical, evolutionary structure of mathematics could be built on geometry, too; and that would be more coherent with the Greek tradition. Still the path leading to computer science has more algebraic background fertilized and mixed with the emergence of logic, as the primary development of Greek philosophy. That is the strong reason for my somewhat turgid addressing of algebra in this context.

Thus, in the evolutionary sequence of computation-related disciplines, we start with algebra. Following the quoted fascinating interpretations, its roots lie in the achievements of numbering and measuring some five million millennia previous. This was the origin of numbers, integers, natural numbers, of the basic relations of addition, subtraction and of the more complex operations: multiplication and division. The whole fundament of algebra can be found in the practical tasks of measuring distances and the scaling and design of architectural constructions. People started to measure time, related to the forecast of natural phenomena and celestial observations; early beginnings of calculating social background for taxation, feeding people, warfare, control of animals, weapons, etc.

2.2.2. COORDINATIZATING...

The development of scaling, coordinatizating, and placing objects in the field of observation generated the further basic number concepts. The integers were soon and naturally extended to rational fractions, as division was needed into parts and later with negative numbers indicating subtraction and opposite direction. The problem of irrational numbers—as the result of plane geometrical problems, triangle, orthogonal structures, the perimeter-diameter relations of the circle—have been difficult obstacles for several hundred years.

The story of numbers as attributes of certain objects and the conceptual abstraction of numbers as some kinds of nouns could be surprisingly observed in the efforts of great thinkers who seem, in terms of intellectual creativity, not at all inferior to us. The clear detachment is not working yet in our common conversation, and it is not necessary but for mathematically and philosophically unsophisticated minds. This is analogous to the distinction problems of mass and weight and several others in physics, and consequently if somebody wants to treat the definitive clarity of further thinking, he/she should try to handle both meanings. The Platonic idea of an abstracted and somehow detached reality and the rigidity of conceptually stubborn, primitive materialism speak both against the creative dual of metaphorical and conceptual generalizations and for the steady feedback principle of abstraction mechanisms. The synchronism of these quasi-parallel processes is a rather loose issue. Our reference can be the theory of electrodynamics and recently the application of number theory for problems of cryptography, the theory of general relativity, and the quantum computational idea of the Hamiltonian *quaternions* (more about this in the next section and in Appendix 2.4).

Algebra represents the course of abstraction. It started with the simplest operations with integers and has now reached the multidimensional algebras of quantum theory and cosmology. The Platonic view of a realistic detached life of these abstracted concepts, even of the integers should not be confused with the conceptual models of more and more complex entities. Aristotle gave a very clear example of the reality-abstraction problem: "We cannot suppose the existence of some house beyond the (existing) houses." The evolutionary development of the conceptual thinking offers a way of understanding this abstraction process. The concept of patterns, used by computer science, is not only a helpful metaphor but strong proof in the factual evolutionary neural history as it was introduced in the first chapter. The final clarification of the puzzle is given in the mechanisms of the brain and how current progress of this fast emerging science test the physiological hypothesis. The far reaching analogies and differences in those physiological and machine processes influence and stimulate not only the general epistemic view but also our computer-modeling development and practice.

Detachment of these abstracted numbers, coordinates and their operations' concepts in the role of mind representations and instruments of thinking is an example of constructing in a skeptical, critical manner. Quoting Wigner (1960): "Mathematical concepts turn up in entirely unexpected connections."

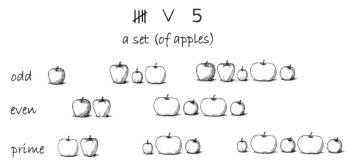

The number concepts —number, even , odd, prime

In this path we can come back to the evolutionary model of conceptual thinking. The buildup of the abstracted conceptual models is a natural representation of experienced descriptions of connections. They are represented and developing in our brains and working in this abstracted world of modeling. Connections are able to construct new hypotheses and various hidden brain and nature-related structures, treated in a later context. The evolutionary brain develops as a representation of experienced conceptual hierarchies and their connectivity mechanisms.

The evolutionary emphasis is not at all an ideological bias for our treatment, though it looks to develop into strong evidence in all kinds of scientific discoveries. Evolution is a complex trend, driven not only by natural selection of competition but also by random variations of the evolutionary material and its environment. The analogy with the evolution of abstracted thinking and in our hypotheses particularly in mathematics is *for me* strong evidence, unlike to the various Platonic ideas. By that, the constructive critical view of our epistemic standpoint receives its practical meaning.

2.2.3. And Coordinatizating Even More...

The Renaissance and furthermore the Age of Reason accelerated the developments of abstraction: numbering more dimensions, beyond the three-dimensional space of everyday geometry. The subsequent revolutionary opening of geometrical-mathematical fantasy in the previous centuries started the conceptual extensions toward multidimensional spaces of physics and several other phenomena.

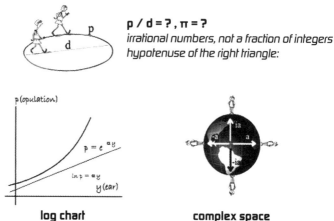

p / d = ? , π = ?
irrational numbers, not a fraction of integers
hypotenuse of the right triangle:

log chart   **complex space**

further representational transformations in the next sections.

Returning to the Age of Reason, the great novelty was the measurement and comparing different interactions for the modern instruments of science. The conceptual world of the Galileian-Newtonian new physics was born in that interaction of measurement, numbering-dimensionalism, and refinement of definitions, e.g., that of mass and power, static and dynamic states.

The need and possibilities of measurement and calculations covered irrational numbers such as π and e. Furthermore, measurements and calculation were able to reconcile problems in the imaginary notation for orthogonal turn in the plane, *quaternion* for orientation in four directions, relative to a certain start 0 (origo), tensor and matrix numbers for multidimensional transformations, groups of functional transformations for phenomena of Hamiltonian motion, relativity, and quantum theory.

The evolution of the number-concept created a structured order shortly reviewed in Appendix 2.4. Each further development contained the previous number class as its subset—each number of higher complexity can be reduced to the lower one if only the expressive power is required within the complexity.

In the opposite direction the correspondence does not work in a similar way. A rather late realization was the nature of the so-called transfinite numbers for different classes of numbers in the world of infinity and where the ordering, the fundamental nature of previous numbers was dubious, too. The problem opened a new stream in the revision of basic definitions, a new chapter of algebraic thinking, a great and stimulating, sometimes polemic debate of the greatest minds in mathematics and philosophy. In the next chapter we return to that discussion and its results for today.

The order had to be restored by a new definition of classes and the evaluation operations on those classes. The original and earlier quoted objective of Galileo: "Measure what is measurable, and make measurable what is not so," was weakened and widened by the thesis of Shafarevich: "When meeting a new type of objects we are forced to construct new types of "quantities" (or, we have to discover them), by which the object can be coordinatized."

These are the conceptual developments of the classic notion of numbers in modern algebra. All these, as the small references of the previous sentence indicate, are rooted in some ways in the advances of the sensory systems and sensory-technology. Advances of the sensory system, instrumentation as conceptual origins of only seemingly detached aspects! Opening a mathematical discussion on infinity and coordinating infinity was a natural but indirect consequence of extending exploration of natural phenomena, of the micro- and macro-world limits.

In this view the intrinsic relation with advancements in physics is not surprising at all. The forming of crystals, the development of geometry, of more and more complex objects in architecture and manufacturing, the *Lagrangean-Hamiltonian* classic and quantum mechanics, the basic *Maxwellian*-electrodynamics and its quantum theory extension, the transformations of general relativity and its relations to gravity, all find appropriate mathematical descriptions and even predictive hypotheses in the instruments of abstract algebra. The way of abstraction follows the relational ways of natural phenomena; abstraction itself is the evolutionary mental development of the more and more complex observational experience, getting acquainted with reality. This can be the explanation of the autonomous development of mathematical concepts, and as referred to earlier, sometimes preceding the applications in science. The posterior applications can be arguments for the hypothesis about the natural development of the conceptual world and not against.

2.2.4. FURTHER TO THE LIMITS OF THE UNLIMITED: INFINITY AND ZERO

The conceptual development of different kinds of numbering evoked not only the further abstractions of elementary operations–addition, subtraction, multiplication, and division–but, as a direct consequence of relations, the notions of identity. Identity is conceived as the expression of self-reproduction and recurrence by operations to the original state. The null and unity concepts had to be related to the problems of infinity: infinity in zero dimension; nonexistence, annihilation, and infinity as the inverse of zero; the infinitely small, decreased in an infinite number of steps. In mathematical physics the Dirac delta, an infinitely great impulse in an infinitely short time could

The zero (origo) and the infinity, by mapping the complex space within and outside the unit circle

be applied as an abstracted representation in an approximative calculation of real, extreme phenomena. After many millennia, the conceptual clarification had to wait until the 19–20th century!

Once more, the disciplinary working of mathematical conceptual fantasy is neither an argument against the relations of reality nor the beautiful game of abstractions. On the bases of evolutionary reality many new variations can spring up, some receiving their model role in development of science, some surviving within the conceptual structure or changing and diminishing with later developments. The evolution of nature itself has several different mechanisms; the survival competition is only one of them, seemingly determinant in the world of living creatures.

Our initial model, the Neumann-Conway *Game of Life* includes these different possibilities, not only for the variations of forms but also for the development of more and more complex rules of form-combinations. The course of algebraic operations preserving the initial axioms is the appropriate example.

As mentioned, the development of the number-concepts runs parallel with the conceptual development of operations. By its very nature, the addition stand in the role of the first and complex infinitesimal operations, linear, stepwise approximations, until the present. Nevertheless, the basics, the two constructive operations with their combinational relations, defined long ago, remained the same, even through their multiple abstracted variations. These relational definitions, their completeness or their partial validity, have a definite role in further qualities. In Appendix 2.5 a bird's-eye-view of basic algebraic concepts, operations and axioms can help the remembrance and understanding of *constrained freedom* within the structure of the game and with the possibilities of reality. This *is the far reaching epistemic moral for all kinds of knowledge structures.*

2.3. Sets, Other Entity Abstractions

> *To see a World in a grain of sand,*
> *And Heaven in a wild flower,*
> *Hold Infinity in the palm of your hand*
> *And Eternity in an hour*
> William Blake, *Auguries of Innocence*

2.3.1. Sets: The Entity Abstraction

We now use the term of sets. On the one hand, in everyday discourse it is a very common word for a combination of pieces, like a set of cosmetics for example. In mathematics, set theory is a fairly recent foundation of the conceptual world, starting with Bolzano in about 1840 and especially with Cantor in 1873. It is related to those highly abstracted structures referred to as number infinity. Our reference is quoted as naïve set theory, reaching the ordinary levels of the everyday discourse.

The prominence of algebra in our context is hopefully clearer by this small, professionally cool detour. This book intends to be a picture of ways of thinking in and for a practical world. The slogan, *nothing is more practical than a good theory*, comes to mind at every turn of abstraction and its feedback.

The algebraic operations stemming from simple calculation tasks received their practical relevance in the combination of more complex entities–different sets of objects and object-related conceptual sets. The addition of two atmospheric streams has more intrinsic sophistication than the addition of two apples, nevertheless, the addition of two bags of apples require an expert check of identity of the brand, maturity etc.

These refinements of set qualities led to the abstractions of algebraic entities and the definitions of the possibilities and limitations of operations within and among certain set classes.

Let us return to the two starting models: the *Game of Life* and the *Turing-machine*. These are the model archetypes, coordinates on the now infinite dimensional checkerboard and an infinitely open hierarchy of moves, i.e. operations. This is all what comprises the activities of computation. The reader can see now the first role of algebra in our considerations: the discipline of stepwise abstracted coordinates, the edifice of numbers.

The second fundamental role of algebra is the discipline of operations–computing itself. This part of the virtual, abstracted, staircase-patterned edifice, or may be, with a more adequate metaphor, scaffolding, is even more fascinating.

Algebra starts with the simplest counting: addition of integers. All operations, used in mathematics and computations are offspring. This is true for the four rules of arithmetic, for the infinitesimal calculi and for all operations computable with advanced linear approximations. No surprise, the twin fundamental models are really valid!

The rules—the possible calculation combinations—follow the same inheritance as it was summed up in Appendix 2.5. The applicability of these calculation combinations is the main characteristic of differences in the classes of algebraic models, i.e., the classes of computational possibilities embodied by algebraic structures. The computational models of these structures are named accordingly, *Boolean, Lie,* etc.

Here we reached the essential computational point: relations of phenomenological models, i.e., models of physical, biological, social and other phenomena, and their relations, are represented by algebraic objects. The computational power of transformations, within and by these structures, creates great avenues and some pitfalls of research, orientation, and design with algebraic methods.

The general procedures are transformations within the constraints of algebraic features. The algebraic model and its transformations express similarities, interactions, resemblances, and correlations—many kinds of design and control activities. The way of application is mostly a turn back to the simplest or best known model of the *class*. From this archetype model, using the permitted transformation procedures, we try to reach the model, which looks to be closest to the case under investigation.

Turning to the basic metaphor and subject of physics, in any problem of motion, we usually start with a representation by the Newtonian equations and proceed further with derived differential equations of energy balances, additional models of friction, turbulence, etc. With the balance equations we find also similarities with other kinds of dynamics, e.g., electrodynamics. The analogous models of rotation also receive some similar model representations and therefore similar algebraic expressions for computation, from the original, simpler, more general model towards the special case of interest.

From the vast mathematical discipline of algebra we recall only a few concepts that represent the structures and their computational procedures used in these transformations—model precisions.

2.3.2. Different Set Classes: Different Conditions of Transformations

The basic distinctions of abstract algebraic set concepts generally do not relate to the qualitative set differences and identities which enable the physical, chemical, or other types of compositions; such is the task of specific professional knowledge. The distinctions concern the computational conditions, especially the main practical virtue of algebra, the possibilities and conditions of transformation. This transformation, if chosen well, based on professional specifics, can express intrinsic relations, e.g., in calculating, forming objects, and relations among object classes, e.g., our examples in meteorology.

From the modeling-computational viewpoint, the transformation operations are our keys. As emphasized, they suggest analogous structures for further ideas and computational instruments for solving specific problems on the basis of some general, possibly simple structures. These transformation operations are the *mappings*–mapping from one structure to another, if the essential structures of the original can be preserved.

The procedures can be visualized for our imagination. We start with a sheet of paper, i.e., mapping in two dimensions, and we try different folding. The next exercise is tessellation or parquetry–covering

Semantics of addition operation

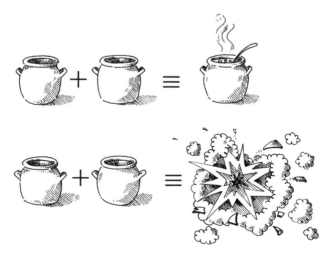

the surface with sheet forms that can be cut from the original sheet and cover the other completely, without waste, overlap, or gap. The following exercise is to do these with elastic sheet material which can be stretched and compressed without tear or protrusion. The exercise can be continued in three dimensions with some plastic material. The next dimensions are committed to more fantasy.

The algebraic mapping enhanced with the optical exercise of projections and lens or mirror operations follow these, mostly visual experiences with a rigor needed for the correct results of abstracted operations and with ingenuity of mathematical imagination. Operations with plastic materials and optical instruments can demonstrate the transformations from linear to non-linear phenomena and vice versa.

The consideration of mapping type constraints starts with the basic algebraic axioms of commutativity, associativity, distributivity, the existence of zero, and unity element, negative and inverse. According to the completeness of these conditions do we have rings, fields, and other structures? The permissible operations conserve those qualities which are important for our model based considerations.

The main computational condition of the algebraic structures differs in commutativity, i.e., in the theoretical-computational possibility of a return cycle and balances. The symmetry features of the sets and their operations are also expressed by these distinctions.

From the epistemic perspective, the axiomatic conditions define the possibilities of model representation. Practically all computable phenomena can be expressed or at least approximated by polynomials. The polynomial representation and its long chained but strict relation to the elementary arithmetic of the Turing-machine prove the deep algebraic constraints of finally digital (Boolean) arithmetic and all steps of intermediate abstractions up to the multidimensional algebras of theories in cosmology and elementary particles.

The chain of computation and its realization in the elementary world of the Turing machine is a real wonder of mathematical construction. Add (and subtract) singular, identical steps and store the result. This, iterated several times, is the mechanism of representation numbers and all arithmetic operations. Linear differential equations—the representations of dynamics—have analogous solutions to arithmetic algebraic equations. Computable nonlinearities can be approximated by singular linearization steps, based also on the same mechanism. As we will see, the system of natural numbers, received at the first step, can represent logical structures and logically constructed algorithms for all these operations.

We instantly understand the main building structure composed from the same simple bricks. How these bricks form a building is the further task of design and realization ingenuity! Installation of this house is a further task, as far as it can be materialized by the same brick components, i.e., by computational instruments. This means that, as far as we use any uncertainty estimations and reasoning methods, we step into the same but very high level algebraic stream.

2.3.3. Mapping, Morphism, Kernels

The projection metaphor helps in understanding the basic concepts of mapping. *Morphism*, the quality of mapping forms and objects concerns the possibility of one-to-one correspondence between the original and the mapped. If the one-to-one correspondence is complete we speak about *isomorphism* and similar conceptual denominations refer to more or less perfect relations.

We can understand that these qualities of correspondences are not only important from an easier or possibly computational point of view but even more so from epistemic similarity hypotheses.

Mapping into–isomorphism

Laminar flow

Turbulent flow

3 D surfaces, their coordinatization and computational modeling via stepwise linearization by projections on tangent planes of partial differentials

The connection of isometric points on a surface or in a higher dimensional space can be transformed into orthogonal, Cartesian coordinate maps and by these operations treated with linear algebras. These methods are best visualized in fluid mechanics. They represent the tangent spaces of the dynamics and, by that, the predictive directions of extrapolated future states.

The projection metaphor and its coordinating relation suggest the *kernel* and *image* concept–a smaller representation of an object via its projections. This is an extended, highly generalized equivalent of a three-dimensional object representation on a two dimensional drafting surface.

Coordinated transformations of the Cartesian orthogonals

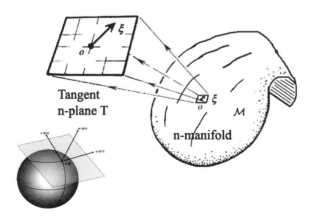

Tangent
n-plane T

n-manifold

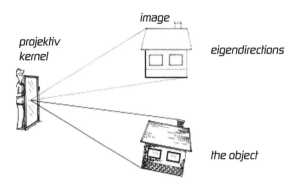

The KERNEL as a magic mirror

Mathematically, the kernel is what we lose or forget when perform a mapping. The image is what remains as a result of the map.

The word, kernel, is used for different concepts in mathematics, too. For example, kernel is the function to be integrated in an equation. As outlined above, the algebraic kernel can be visualized by projections, skeletonizing, and as an operator. The result of the operation is the image, and let us recall, what was said about non-linear, multidimensional mapping: the kernel can be a complex functional operator, too. A kernel function under an integral operator represents a filling up of a space outlined by the kernel.

These concepts are important instruments in all kinds of computational problems. If we would like to characterize any factual or virtual object, in search of determinant components, looking for similar solutions weakening or strengthening some values or side effects, recognizing an object or situation based on some hypotheses and previous knowledge—finally we use these projective ideas, conceptual and related computational means.

The widely applied optimization tasks apply similar procedures, and most of the enumerated problems are reduced to some kind of optimization, too. Support vector methods, simulated annealing approximations, adaptive control, and pattern recognition by mapping are all based on these. The alien-looking statistical-probabilistic methods, like application of Markovian chains, Monte-Carlo methods (see Appendix 2.6) and all others can in the final analysis be reduced to algebraic origins.

Why to emphasize these origins so much? Why are the well applied and computationally supported procedures enough for any advanced application? The main reason lies in the underlying way of thinking: the constructive, creative procedure from the very beginnings, thousands of years before computers. People worked and reasoned in these pattern-mapping ways. They applied and boosted admirable ingenuity, were within their environment practical and usable, but they also consolidated false solutions, manners, and rites, especially if the original environmental conditions changed. All novelties of mathematics and computer science are continuations and mappings on a very high abstraction avenue of modeling. The pitfalls due to this elongated way of modeling are more imminent than ever, especially in our times as disciplinary continuity is mostly broken due to the specialization requirements of sophisticated modern science-based technologies. It is elongated by the complexity of the task and related technologies, by their mathematical formulations, by programming the models and executing the programs, finally by interpretation and implementation of the computer given results. The other reason of increased epistemic criticism is our valuable success story, the application of modeling methods in human behavior-related problems of technological control, as well financial and social-psychological behavior with weaknesses of related knowledge.

2.3.4. SPACES, OPERATORS

Operation with numbers started with addition. Once more, we come back to the earthy basement of high algebra. The development of calculation with algebraic entities was step-by-step simultaneous with the development of operations: arithmetic, differential, Boolean-logical, and linear combinations with matrices. Further developments included the achievements of general theories of *operators*, functions, functions of functions, functionals, and all kinds of transformation, mapping operations on all kinds of algebraic, topological spaces. The concept of topological spaces is also a theoretically abstract and practically useful idea. In topological spaces the union and intersection of all elements belong to the same space, i.e. the algebraic compositions and operations permit similar qualities. The

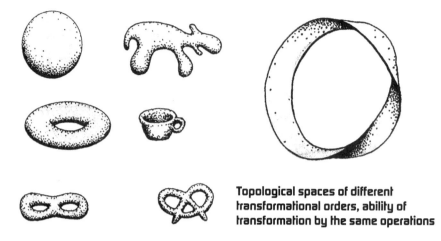

Topological spaces of different transformational orders, ability of transformation by the same operations

visual metaphor helps in understanding how these topological spaces are bound to certain operations with certain algebras.

If we know all about the space of the problem, e.g., that it is continuous without having some singularities, such as a flowing stream without turbulent regions, we can select the operator for mapping and look for a convenient solution for our recognition and navigation task. Let us continue the case: navigation on a river that has a gentle bend and slower flow, due to more free space. The geographical space can be mapped by simple differential and matrix operators to a space of flow velocities, and the two combined to a space of arrival times. The situation is much more complicated if the river meets a region where a rocky island breaks the flow into several turbulent streams of different length and width. The space of the river changes in its character, mathematically, the *homology*–the uniform regularity characteristic of the space–is broken, as well as the validity of earlier applied algebra and related operators.

The homology conditions demonstrate well the deep relation between epistemic nature and applicable algebras. The simplest example is frequently cited: to form a simple cup from any plastic mass requires one type of shaping operation, to add a handle from the same mass needs a separate one, e.g., punching a hole.

The situation can be worse. The well coordinated map can be spoiled in an unknown region, and the regular coordination returns

| Program | algebraic | program | visual |

Packages representation

only after that space. The experienced navigator fixes the two end-points of the regular regions and starts experimentations with other navigational search operators such as radars and orientation poles. The mathematician does the same, using the known coordinates as *factors* in the row of known integers and orders of magnitude as logarithmically ordered milestones and starts a search within the unknown range of *moduli*, randomly as in the Monte Carlo method, or by stepwise approximation, or looking for some recurrent regularities by the means of periodic operators (Fourier, fractal, wavelet, or similar). Surfers in a turbulent, high running flow exercise the same: they try to learn and adjust themselves to the periodic waveforms. Once more, searching, learning, and adjustment for and by operators is the task, operators for the hypothetical space structures.

The available conceptual hierarchy advances very far. Similar operators create structures, structures of operators, *classes*, all define their own algebras, i.e., their computational rules and programmable procedures. This way, all computable functions, and by them all computable models, can be classified into the theoretically beautiful conceptual matryoshka dolls. What is more, the structures yield practical recommendations for the use of the appropriate mathematical model instrument, and for program synthesis, through commercially and freely available programming tools.

2.4. Algebraic Operations in Highly Practical Roles: Computational Classes

And wisely tell what hour o' th' day
The clock does strike, by algebra
Samuel Butler: *Hudibras I/125*

2.4.1. SOME EPISTEMICALLY AND PRACTICALLY RELEVANT ALGEBRAS

For the illustration of the above, see three especially relevant algebras:
– The transformation algebra of geometry;
– The Boolean algebra of logic;
– The Lie algebra of transformations, especially related to phenomena of physics and physics-related analogy models.

Further, there are two relevant applications as selected examples:

2.4.2. EUCLIDEAN GEOMETRY

Visual origins of thinking are rooted in associative abstraction of forms, being more characteristic for identities and differences than other sensory impressions. This is a rather sweeping statement against the decisive role of color, smell, and audio sensitivity of different living creatures. Structured relations of those either don't exist or are at least much less developed than those of visual forms. Verbal abstraction is also based on form structures. The development of color and olfactory characteristics give evidence to this hypothesis.

Geometry is the offspring science of forms, especially of forms created by the progress of the *homo faber*. The other line of abstraction was a more complex and less structured conceptual world of intra-human and human nature relations, leading to different levels of metaphysics. Both conceptual developments were and are present in all civilizations, though their role and maturity differ significantly. The rather unique phenomena of the antique Greek civilization and much later in the Age of Reason appeared in several respects in our explanations. This first led to the still flourishing heritage of the Euclidean geometry, the second period of the unfolding of mathematical physics. The relevant feature behind these is the practical, utility-driven rational attitude of these civilizations. The changing pressures of these utility rationales and the adverse social binding powers of many-sided conservations decided the ups and downs of civilizations in the long range and in the shorter periods as well.

Another quotation from Volterra, an ingenious Italian mathematician, as he denied taking an oath on the fascist empire: "Empires die, but Euclid's theorems keep their youth forever."

The Euclidean heritage is surviving not only in the discipline of elementary geometry but also in its strong definition-proof structures and in all further developments, named usually non-Euclidean, but really being far-reaching logical descendants. The reunification of mathematics with geometry, the *analytic geometry* was probably the most durable achievement of the whole Cartesian oeuvre. According to Hawking, Isaac Newton could never have founded his laws without the analytic geometry of René Descartes and Newton's own invention of calculus. We usually say now that Euclidean geometry and Newtonian physics are "only" approximations of the Riemannian geometry and Einsteinian physics, but the opposite formulation is equally true, algebraically spoken this statement is commutative: how we think now is a straight generalization of the Euclidean-Newtonian world view. This is valid in the perspective of ways of thinking in conceptual visual imagination and in ways of mathematical rigor.

The development of geometry by extensions via new conceptual definitions and the same process of representation phenomena in physics are parallel proceedings. They reflect the conceptual process of world-model developments.

A further important encounter of geometric and algebraic, number-related thinking is the theory and practice of groups. *Group theory* started with the problem of solving algebraic equations, why equations of higher order than four cannot have explicit, general solutions, similar to linear, quadratic, third and fourth order equations? The problem is highly practical—remember the computational problems of polynomial expressions and the similarity in solving differential equations in any dynamic model. Theoretical investigation led the fantastic and short-lived Galois to formulate the modern theory of groups. Groups are entities whose elements can be multiplied with each other.

Multiplication is a binary operation that is associative and admits an identity element. The elements of a group have a multiplicative inverse. These more exact definitional conditions of a group cover the conditions of chaining and conversion of real, materialized elements.

At this exceptionally relevant development let us return to the *Game of Life*. The elementary components can be composed by elementary rules. The evolution of rules was mentioned as a further step in evolution of structures. Here we are, the combinational possibilities and restrictions of algebraic structures are the descendant rules for more complex phenomena. Illustrating these, let us draw the attention to the fast evolving knowledge about the molecular combination, their generative and inhibitory features representing a basic level of all life phenomena.

The mapping problem of numbers, equations, anything expressed by those, belonging or not belonging to the same group of phenomena is *a* or *the* general epistemic problem of science and science-based modeling. It is a problem of evolution and further of possibilities of creating molecular and atomic structures, reaching similar or dissimilar effects in pharmacology and all fields of biology. It refers to the ways of creative thinking, rational reasoning and free associations.

The mapping problem, in its visual metaphors, is living in the world of geometrical structures. Symmetry, kinds, and numbers of symmetries—possibilities of covering spaces with groups of components—lead to the existence and possibilities of regularities, expressed first of all by geometry and used in architecture, crystallography, material sciences, nuclear physics, cosmology, and arts.

The refinement of the conceptual world of these groups and schemes did not happen quickly—their definitional accuracy received their matured form in the 20th century only, by Noether and several other algebraists of that highly abstracted field.

This late history is surprising for all external observers of mathematics, concerning the very ancient origins of this science. The refinement of homology-transformation concepts, limits and capabilities cannot be explained by the computational revolution, i.e., by the direct influence of applications in complex geometry-related programs. The process can be viewed as a mutual and mostly indirect interaction of thinking about the computability of the ever increasing number and complexity of observational data, requirements of difficult engineering design, the modeling trends of social and economic phenomena, and the endeavor for an overall general mathematical-logical interpretation of the rational in the universe.

The progress evoked a renewed marriage of geometry, geometric interpretations, and other branches of mathematics by and for new interpretation models of physics and all kind of dynamics in nature and human relations. That was the advent of the current level of mathematical-computational modeling in most natural sciences and sciences considered soft.

The story—the immediate anticipation of computational revolutions—can be a challenging subject for deeper research in the

Some further transformations, various surfaces, objects, all by programmed mathematical representations

```
> J:=Jacobian(ti,[x,y,z]);
> lindiff:=Matrix(eval(J,{x=p0[1],y=p0[2],z=p0[3]}));
> tl:=(u,v,w)->convert(lindiff.Vector([u,v,w]),list);
> evalf(tl(0,0,0));
> evalf([t1(p0[])]);
> linapp:=map(c->evalf(i0+tl((c-p0)[])),circum):
> display(plot3d([bl],x=-1.2..1.2,y=-1.2..1.2,axes=normal),
```

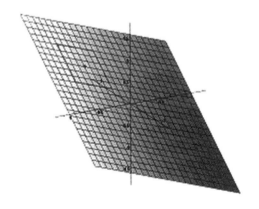

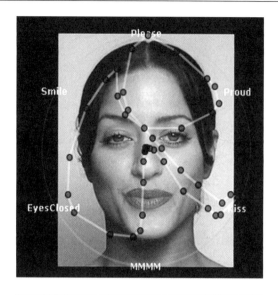

development of human thinking. The lesson is an orientation with respect to the results, and is an otherwise hardly attainable special knowledge of those who offer more advanced computational tools. One of these virtues is the appreciation of basics and the continuous revision of applicability, modeling limits. All this makes us return to the start, the critical requirements of knowledge about knowledge, now in geometry, technological transformations and morphological analysis of shapes, and all related problems connected to geometrical entities and analogies.

Returning to the origins, another but not diverging view:

Algebraic geometry is a mixture of the ideas of two Mediterranean cultures. It is the superposition of the Arab science of the lightning calculation of the solution of equations over the Greek art of position and shape. This tapestry was originally woven on

European soil and is still being refined under the influence of international fashion. Algebraic geometry studies the delicate balance between the geometrically plausible and the algebraically possible. Whenever one side of this mathematical teeter-totter outweighs the other, one immediately loses interest and runs off in search of a more exciting amusement. (Kempf, 1993)

2.4.3. BOOLEAN ALGEBRA

We can tell a similar story about binary Boolean algebra, first named as an algebra by Boole himself. From an algebraic point of view, we find a *ring* of two integers, the ominous *zero,* and *one,* in roles very close to their algebraic interpretations, and as rules of Boolean logic, all operations of the *field*, and therefore of a *commutative ring*. Catching a ring only, a short entertaining review is given in Appendix 2.5.

Simple problems of Boolean logic don't necessitate the delicacies of the above very general relations. The validity of Boolean rationale is always endangered by the validity of the initial statements, the premissae, and not less by the further conditions of the binary nature of the phenomena under discussion. This complex problem leads to related questions about classic probability theory.

The proliferation of bifurcations and ramifications of consequences, the introduction of uncertainty estimates, the influence of mutual influences and nets excluded in the original postulates, led readily to more complex models. These cannot be reviewed by a clever eye but can be filtered and analyzed by some computational methods.

The ramifications provoke the development of graph representations and their theory about graphs. The yes-no decisions lead to big trees and nets of possibilities and impossible solutions, the science of choosing better or worse roots. Several graph-search algorithms offer faster and reasonable solutions and therefore they have well developed methodologies for machine reasoning and artificial intelligence algorithms.

We return to these in chapters about logic and uncertainty, approximations and computability. The only purpose of the present discussion is to show the practical aspects of the most general philosophical-mathematical frame of algebra, once again *thinking about thinking*.

2.4.4. Lie Groups

One of the most useful branches of algebra is the fast developing application of Lie groups. The original algebraic idea is the algebraic application of mathematical operations, especially of differential and integral calculus, i.e., the infinitesimal operations. These operations are the keys for dynamic analysis of physical and other real-life phenomena, mechanics, electrodynamics, electronics, chemistry and biochemistry, and further dynamics of social co-existence. The idea goes back to the algebraic ways to solve differential equations, as referred to in this chapter earlier, to the achievements of the 18th century, and the present applications that were initiated in the 19th century by Lagrange, Hamilton, Cayley, Lie and others.

The essential physical meaning is best represented in the Hamiltonian equations of motion, describing the balances of transitions, and through them the fundamental equilibria of Nature. The Hamiltonian equations are comprised of the transition of potential energy to the energy of motion and vice versa, and leads to the universal formulae of relativity, but first, to the problems of unbalances manifested in the difference form of the *Poisson-bracket* formula of Lie algebras.

Appendix 2.7 provides a short insight on Lie groups and Lie algebras.

2.5. Two Examples

> *Das wird nächstens schon besser gehen,*
> *Wenn ihr lernt Alles reducieren*
> *Und gehörig klassificieren*
>
> *Next time, be sure, you will have more success,*
> *When you have learned how to reduce*
> *And classify all by its use*
>
> Johann Wolfgang von Goethe, *Faust*

2.5.1. Pattern Recognition

Pattern recognition is one of the widest application areas, ranging from recognition of objects, working environments for robots, recognition of people, their interior and exterior body features, gestures, voice, signatures for medical purposes and for more human communication and security, recognition of natural and artificial areas for improving agriculture, water management, for all kinds of geographic applications, traffic control, observations of mass and rapid phenomena in particle physics, reaction chemistry, and astronomy. And we did not completely exhaust the realm of applications!

The pattern recognition process

The pattern recognition process usually starts with the recognition of the line segments and/or with recognition of well separable surface parts with geometrical coordination. Kernel methods are used frequently. As was mentioned, the kernels reduce the dimensions to be treated and, if they are directed to characteristic features, they can underline similarities and differences. The search for eigendirections skeletonizes the problem.

From the very beginning of computer technology philosophers discussed the meaning of the word *understanding* as the definitive proof for machine abilities. In my understanding, the recognition of a picture means the understanding of that, if not totally. *Not totally*, because the expert steps further in his/her knowledge base. How far and what this means from a fundamental point of view is the further subject.

2.5.2. Meteorology

For measuring the state of a certain area of the atmosphere, a spatial net is defined for the points of measurement.

The aggregate of these points is the *field* of the space. In this context field means, first of all, the subject of discourse and research and not the field of algebra. If we go further, the coordinatization task emerges, and for that and for the following mathematical-computational treatment the investigated regions should be identified from the point of view of algebraic models. Each point is coordinatized by its geographical and height position, temperature, pressure, humidity and other components, solid particles included, and six degrees of freedom of translational and rotational wind velocity, i.e., much more than ten data define the individual points of multidimensional space. The transformation of this space is the matter of forecast. The transformation is described by the chain of transformational matrices of differential operators and groups—mostly Lie groups—expressing the transformational image of the changing data, movement, and other states of the atmosphere. The application of Lie algebra expresses also the non-uniform, nonlinear nature of the atmospheric space. In the *Poisson bracket* the asymmetry is measured and it provides a key for the further investigation of the causes of irregularities, e.g., turbulence, local streams, chemical reactions, electrical discharges, and

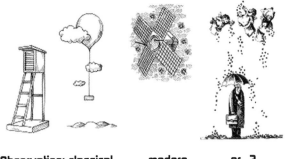

Observation: classical, modern or...?

main directions of changes. The reduced two dimensional spaces of different streams were illustrated in this chapter earlier. The multidimensional, dynamic, nonlinear space of meteorology, along with many further effects—among others the ocean jet streams—create immense data structures and transformation modeling Lie operator matrices of meteorological computation.

These two examples are only brute simplifications and extractions of the extremely elegant representational, computational power of modern algebra.

2.6. Abstracted Reality: Reflections in the Brain and Résumé

nihil in intellectu nisi prius in sensu
(nothing in the intellect unless first in sense)
Empiricist maxim quoted frequently and attributed to many

2.6.1. ALGEBRA HIDDEN IN THE BRAIN?

How deeply the intrinsic structural world of the brain is related to mathematical relations is best exemplified by some surprising achievements of art. The aesthetic urge followed the history of all civilizations from the beginnings.

The Egyptian-Troian art could represent a nearly complete sequence of a special group transformation and many later *architectural forms* and *tapestry figures* reflect that limited multitudes of group-symmetry transformations.

**The Egyptian-
Troian art**

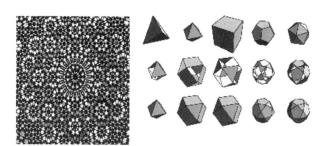

tapestry figures   **Platonic bodies**

The symbolic power and relevance of the *Platonic bodies* has a similarly long history. They have interesting roles in theoretical physics, just recently completed by a most complex eight symmetric geometry body: the E_8. Just how complex E_8 is can be revealed in the following quote:

> This achievement is significant both as an advance in basic knowledge and because of the many connections between E_8 and other areas, including string theory and geometry. The magnitude of the calculation is staggering: the answer, if written out in tiny print, would cover an area the size of Manhattan. Mathematicians are known for their solitary work style, but the assault on E_8 is part of a large project bringing together 18 mathematicians from the U.S. and Europe for an intensive four-year collaboration....The result of the E_8 calculation, which contains all the information about E_8 and its representations, is 60 gigabytes in size. *http://www.aimath.org/E8/*

The mathematical proof of those complex patterns, especially of their uniqueness, is mostly an effort of one or two generations and can be understood only by a few devoted algebraists and logicians. However, somewhere in the brain these highly complex structural relations are somehow

**architectural
forms**

Escher-transformations

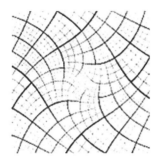 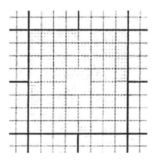

Print Gallery (Prententeenoous constelling)

present, imprinted during many millennia of natural observation and further, memory-based prototype abstractions. No firm localization or mechanism structure has been proven and most probably, similar to other inherited abilities, this capacity is not a readymade structure in the newborn brain. The ability of development, even in a more advanced state, talent-like endowments should be existing, similar to other abilities like learning languages, executing harmonic movements, and dedicated recognition capacities.

Recognition of faces follow this bottom up, top down procedure, a little bit like the sketch of a human body, a head-like oval and the placing of eyes with their aesthetic-emotional specifics. The top-down, bottom-up procedure can be—partly and still now, to a very brute degree—followed

Non-chaotic

chaotic

trajectories generated by a pendulum details

by brain imaging. Best followed in the retina-visual cortex cooperation, it works simultaneously in both directions, in an also memorized optimal looking to and fro sequence, somehow similar to pattern abstraction.

That was the story of the Bach-structures and *Escher-transformations*, especially of the *Print Gallery (Prententeenoous constelling)* composition, and of those graphics analyzed by Hofstadter (1979), and later by Hendrik Lenstra (2002) and others, in computing the hidden message of the enigmatic center of the picture.

Pollock: Number 14

The abstract pictures, with a random splatter of Pollock hide deep fractal relations—Pollock was honing his fractals a quarter of a century before they were defined (*Nature*, February 7, 2006, pp. 648-649).

Two remarks to this sensational finding: Fractals were well known by mathematicians much before the naming by Mandelbrot (1977, 1982). Weierstrass could be the first, in 1872, followed by many others. The other remark relates to the mathematical rigor of the concept. Fractals in their strong definition can be continued without limit into similar smaller figures; the Pollock structures have only a limited similarity extent. To this idea, as mentioned, Escher puzzles are more similar to fractals.

The other end, Mondrian's geometric structures reflect a special order of beauty, remembrance to the fascinating aesthetic impressions of all great compositions. All these structures most likely receive a resonance, hidden in our brains—the adopted structures of Nature.

Further, the same regularity—algebra of Nature—can be found nearly everywhere.

Symmetries and algebraic-looking composition-interaction rules regulate the strictly limited numbers of crystal structure transformations and forms on living creatures.

Folding in two dimensions for three dimensional objects is not only a nice game, like origami, but also a developmental feature of nature, e.g., in cylindrical or helical plants, like pine cones and pineapples, or flowers. They are also used for modern ways of packaging. This is a special mathematics of structural relations. (*Nature*, July 26, 2007, p. 419.)

Quantum mechanics and the further standard models of elementary particles offer deep evidence for the model of a limited number of initial components. They have a limited number of intrinsic qualities for possible and for excluded interactions. The model and behavior of the stem cell in biology looks similar to the picture of evolutionary development.

The problem of the hidden Lie symmetries was mentioned in this chapter earlier, another interesting communication about the ways of thinking by the ingenious physicist Dirac. Most of his achievements were in the abstracted world of algebra but according to his interview with Thomas Kuhn, his approach was fundamentally geometrical, i.e. inspired by visual fantasy ("Dirac's Hidden Geometry," *Nature* Sept. 15, 2005, p. 323).

The cosmological reference drives back to the debated first few seconds or milliseconds of the universe, i.e., the border of the mystical and metaphysical, and is really a problem challenging theoretical speculations but it does not disturb the modeling view of algebraic abstraction-reality. According to Wittgenstein: "There is indeed the inexpressible. This shows itself: it is the mystical," (*Tractatus*, 6.522) and his answer was thus: "It is not how things are in the world that is mystical, but that it exists" (6.44).

Allusions to the brain mechanisms reflect all recent advances of experimental biology on the one hand and the majority of conclusions and hypotheses on the other. In my view and in the spirit of this essay, they strengthen the monistic, evolutionary interpretations and by these a rather transparent working model both for research and for the constructive feature of obligatory skepticism.

The strong evidence of this fundamental relation: the atomistic elements (in the ancient Greek philosophical sense) and their basic interaction rules create the infinite variations of natural structures, and our brain's ways of thinking as well. These few basic rules proliferate into the creation of mental structures in question and into the finitude and other kinds of limitations of all further phenomena.

The interpretation problem has a long discussed binary root. This is the top-down thinking from a teleological, principally purpose-directed point of view, or bottom-up, progressing in a certain logical sequence. Noether, one of the deepest thinkers and mathematicians of the 20th century, proved that both ways can be effective and lead to the same result but they cannot be mixed and confused. The two are logically, in this case philosophically, different. This essay follows the bottom-up logic of science.

Returning to the initial models, the *Game of Life* and the *Turing-machine*, the way of developing more and more complex rules looks to be a partially solved problem. Behind this evolutionary process lie the developments of forbidden and preferred ramifications on the development graphs. The axioms of algebra and their consequences in structure specifics are relevant but presumably not complete answers. Fundamental relations of biological interactions can hide the same questions.

From our pragmatic, computational considerations, this two-faced feedback structure—the constructive logic of structural model development and the questioning of nature at each hypothetical step, i.e., the requirement of epistemic feedback—is the main lesson. The mathematical-computational science of structures is and will be powerful support in creating hypotheses, metaphoric representations, and in solving future problems of research technology. The two are not detached and even less so are the ramifications from and to science and humanistics. These ideas are summed up in the following concluding remarks. I refer here, once more, to the scheme of the epistemic feedback loop in the first Section, to the assiduous constructive skeptic feedback of research.

2.6.2. Concluding Lesson

The infinite thread of abstraction indicates a hypothetical order of mathematical world-interpretation. We have to emphasize, again and again, that this hypothetical order is really a subjective viewpoint, but objective in the sense of mirroring, reflection in a certain direction of brain activity.

In this view, algebra is the origin of further fundamentals, created somehow later in the development of thinking: logic, algorithmics, number theory, and all other branches of mathematics, developed in the course of evolutionary abstraction, though are interpreted in different disciplinary ways.

The algebraic origin of number concepts was dealt with. The regularities and irregularities, the apparent and hidden structures of numbers, are the subject of number theory, which is now a practical and deeply investigated branch of mathematics, also oriented towards computer science.

The foresight does not refer only to the current use in cryptography, saving privacy, property, personal and common security, or applications of opposite intensions. The search towards hidden relations, interactions in data about all kind of phenomena, practical life activities, biological-medical interactions are promising research topics.

This kind of simplistic reasoning should not serve any purpose other than adding a thread to an organic evolutionary view of our science—solidification of the conscious coherence of our epistemic knowledge with the reflected reality. All this speaks against any kind of anti-science movements either from the corner of mysticism, metaphysics or from the other end: from the primitive pragmatism of a narrow business orientation. Both are imminent dangers to present research.

From the point of view of computer science the role in modeling is a relevant issue. In constructing model groups and classes of phenomena, the essential problem is the validity of classifications, the homomorphism among proven and hypothetical models. The algebraic analysis of these structural model relations provides a key for the modeling process, following the sketched evolutionary build-up and similarity features within the group.

2.6.3. HOMAGE TO MATH AND PHYSICS

The other aspect is the more sophisticated pragmatic relevance of mathematics, the distilled structures of our knowledge, owing to the possibilities of getting to new knowledge in a nature-similar, naturally reduced way. Along this line of thought lies computer science, the mathematics-given vehicle. In this statement physics and physics-originated technology are not forgotten. Mathematics is the language of physics, and via computation, engineering and all other sciences, create a necessary unity-trinity of these epistemic endeavors.

That conclusion is a kind of catechism for those who would like to devote their efforts to the real *pragma* of search: *without having a general glance at this certain universe, the individual paths of the search are more risky.*

2.6.4 Review from Computer Science

From the view of computer science, algebra means the discipline of well-defined algorithmic operations on well-defined structures (rings, groups, sets, etc.). The algorithmic operations are now mostly ready-made programs of mathematical operations, e.g., programs in *Mathematica, Mathlab,* and elsewhere.

Computer science is an excellent example of how abstract branches of science, only seemingly of theoretical interest, start to be practical tools of everyday life. Some parts of that praxis—e.g., solving problems of simpler tasks in coordinate geometry—were applied long ago, but the general use of the beauties of algebra, their refined abstractions, were beyond any practical considerations.

Now, the definitions of *homomorphism* and *isomorphism* are guides to the optimally applicable computational algorithms, e.g., for applying kernel methods in a broad sense, and for solving complex problems expressed or physically related to geometric interpretations. These kernel methods highlight the invariant, structural features which are varied by the functional operations of the model expression.

Typical examples are oceanography, geology, meteorology, structures of solids, and elementary particles—nets of logical and random phenomena. These similarity and identity relations are the mathematical abstractions of the *model* idea.

Algebra is now the science of structural relations and their algorithmic computational approximations, similar to its origins, when it was the know-how of elementary calculus. Algebra, in its abstraction beauty and overall mathematical-structural potential, represents an essential course in ways of rational thinking and, by these double virtues, a lesson for the acknowledgement of the majesty of sciences in general.

CHAPTER 3

Logic, the Origin of All Programming

Mein theuerer Freund, ich rath euch drum
Zuerst Collegium Logicum.

I counsel you, dear friend, in sum
That first you take collegium logicum
Johann Wolfgang von Goethe, *Faust*

3.1. Basic Problems

3.1.1. MATHEMATICS OR PHILOSOPHY?

The question of mathematics or philosophy is not new and not a formal disciplinary classification problem. Logic, as it was born, belonged to philosophy, not only because all science belonged to philosophy. Logic was a major achievement in the first Age of Reason, that of the Greeks, an insight and simultaneously an external view of perception, understanding the order of the world and of the mind in both mental and verbal representations. Maybe this was not conceptualized in that way, not even by the greatest philosophers of the age, but essentially, this is how it happened. Reading their works, we may suppose this heroic height of consciousness.

The answer is valid even in our days. In the duality of thinking about the world and its representation techniques, the epistemic critic of those techniques is included. This essay goes around just that duality and returns several times to the evolutionary nature of the two, as their binding, separate but mutual, asymmetric control. Logic, as mathematics, is an abstracted mechanism, mostly independent from content. This kind of purified mechanism for human and machine thinking has a special value, like the science of numbers, detached from the semantic content of the numbered objects.

The philosophy of logic is for us, in the complexity of computational tasks, an instrument of critique about the validity of mechanized inference, a semantic check of correct applications. Appendix 3.1 summarizes some basic definitions and notations.

3.1.2. ANYTHING NEW, AFTER SYLLOGISMS AND NOTATIONS?

A superficial and critical observer could say: in logic nothing really applicable is new under the sun from the times of ancient Greek science. In his paper "On Mathematical Logic," Skolem, one of the great personalities of modern logic, wrote the following: "Logic, as is well known, was established as a science by Aristotle. Everyman knows the Aristotelian syllogism. During the entire Middle Ages Aristotle's syllogistic figures constituted the principal content of logic. Kant is said to have remarked that logic was the only science that had made no progress at all since antiquity. Perhaps this was true at the time, but today it is no longer so."

Heijenoort, in the preface to his great collection *From Frege to Gödel*, offers a further perspective on logic in history:

> The second half of the nineteenth century saw the rebirth of logic. That science—which, many felt, had reached its completion and lacked any future—entered a renaissance that was to transform it radically. Though it had been heralded by Leibniz the new development did not actually start till the middle of the nineteenth century. Boole, De Morgan and Jevons are regarded as initiators of modern logic, and rightly so. The first phase, however, suffered of a number of limitations. It tried to copy mathematics, too closely, and often artificially. The multiplicity of interpretations of what became Boolean algebra created confusion and for a time was a hindrance rather than an advantage. Considered by itself, the period would, no doubt, leave its mark upon the history of logic, but it would not count as a great epoch.
>
> A great epoch in the history of logic did open in 1879, when Gottlob Frege's *Begriffsschrift* was published. This book freed logic from an artificial interrelation with mathematics, but at the same time prepared a deeper interrelation between these two sciences. It presented to the world in full fledged form, the propositional calculus and quantification theory. (Heijenoort, 1962)

A small but important remark: nobody and nothing exists without relevant ancestors, neither before nor after the Boolean period. Some of the forefathers were mentioned in 2.1.5, now only Leibniz's *Calculus Philosophicus* or *Racionator* should be referred to.

The above quotation is also an example of the different views about the relations of mathematics and logic as a part of philosophy. The age of computers renewed these interrelations and an illustration of those is the endeavor of this chapter.

The Mephistophelian irony is that the basic computer linguistic notation form, the *Backus-Naur* form is reminding some authors of a similar linguistic definition formulae used by Panini (Kapoor, 2005), a scholar of the Indian Antiquity. Several other notational initiatives can be discovered from that period and later in Persian science. We can meditate on why the formal representation of semantics appeared earlier than the representation of grammar, analyzing their historical and cultural reasons.

That happened contemporaneously with Greek science, perhaps a bit earlier, as the other intellectual wonder emerged in India, related to the definition problems of the Sanskrit language. The two origins, one relating to geometry—i.e., to practical problem-solving in the Mediterranean civilization—and the other, relating to language, remained a closely interwoven problem of sources over the next two and a half millennia of development.

According to references, the Sanskrit text is processed phoneme by phoneme to words of the lexicon which contains the rules of a grammatical parser. About 4,000 rules and grammatical, phonetic notations are used in a literal notational order of the linguistic hierarchy, not different from any modern natural text processing analyzer.

Panini used metarules, recursive structures and notational symbols. His contributions were duly acknowledged by most pioneers of modern linguistic theories, notably Saussure and Chomsky. What are advertised as achievements of computer language ontology are not much more than these sophisticated origins.

The possibility that a Natural Language (NL) parser based on Panini's scheme can help to analyze Indian languages has gained momentum in recent years.

These statements can be criticized as being reductionist and biased as some other similar references in this work, but essentially, the problem of continuities and discontinuities, rupture and acceleration periods remain the main subject of research and ways of thinking about values, pedagogy, forgetting, transformations, and preservation.

Regarding the Mephistophelian remark, the intentional relativity of these views, historical analogies, recurrences, even retro fashions, should be considered. Either the emphasis and demonstrational intention are focused on the continuity and cyclic nature of returning ideas, or on the revolutionary novelties and essential differences between the earlier and the current ages. The personal philosophy of this essay tries to maintain some balance, just by its evolutionary view. Evolution is really a process of continuity in a constructive manner and creating new variations with surprising novelties. Our two foundational metaphors, the Game of Life and the Turing machine, both produce these, in creation of new structures and new rules, all based on starting elements. The biological lesson shows how ancient peptides, working in primitive digestive functions, receive new high-level roles in the activity of the brain.

The methods of basic linguistic analysis are not different from that learned in the very traditional grammar curricula of the very traditional grammar schools. The lexical forms are essentially the same as in most traditional major dictionaries. The hyperstructures of the text search, understanding, and composition are the achievements of modern computational linguistics. They apply the structural order and search methods of graph theory, sophisticated statistics and probability relations, semantic and pragmatic schemes of cognitive patterns. We come back to these in the next chapter. The latter methods try to simulate the human ways of cognition: mapping the received information to previously learned phrases, both situations experienced and those stored in the memory. The mechanisms of associations and similarities use thesaurus-like conceptual structures and distance measures based on subjective and statistical estimates, script-like patterns of situations, ideas of groups, and transformations elaborated in algebra. All these associative memory relations or their vague conceptual mechanisms were familiar in ways of thinking, the great novelties are the technological and mathematical-programming inspirations which enable the machines to handle never-before conceivable amounts of information and data.

In fact, if we scrutinize the structures of computer languages and even the hardware primitives of any technology, we find no more than the basic syllogisms of first-order logic and their further nota-tional extensions in the form of instruction primitives. Admirable are the witty, sophisticated ideas of extremely high-complexity com-puting. In fact, usual statements about embedded functions need higher order logic but the programming practice of logical program-ming resolves these into first-order sequences. For example, in the sentence: *People don't buy high-consumption cars,* the embedded statement is resolved to the definition of high consumption and this value is set into the statement about buyers' logic.

The regrettable and admirable truth is not too far from these statements. Admirable because similar to all other complex evolu-tionary systems, the expressive and problem-solving power of the extensions developed through many hierarchical generations, and create an infinite world of situations and state descriptions. The best and most common analogy is the natural language with its phonetic vocabulary, syntactic hierarchy, and expressive power. Logical con-structs of programs develop, as it was only rather illustrated, mod-eling on the same lines, syntax included. This hard analytical and syntactic consequence was consolidated and canonized by the nota-tional progress of the 19th and early 20th centuries.

In the above considerations the roles and disciplines of math-ematical logic, computer programming and linguistics look to be rather confused, not to mention the philosophical and other, cultur-al-historical, representational depths and varieties of linguistics. This is not by chance. The problem covers all aspects of communication and human thinking. The individual threads of development depend on the historical, cultural, and social requirements and means of communication technology. All these received an integral opportu-nity and necessity in our computer-communication age.

3.1.3. The Truth Problem

The conflict of the admirable and regrettable evolved in the same period. The admiration of logic led to the *Russellian-Hilbertian* pro-gram of the universal scientific language, the great tree structure of all *true* knowledge. The story is extensively outlined in several excel-lent books (Chaitin, 2006; Davis, 1965; Heijenoort, 1967; Hilbert and Bernays, 1934–39; Kneale and Kneale, 1962; Russell, 1956).

The concept of truth runs on the same rails with a firm belief that all should be a conceivable, even seizable reality in nature and even in human relations. The change of thinking started with the understanding of limits of logic-created worlds, the curious existence of different extensions of infinity, complexity, and computability. The hypothesis of all these uncertainties about truth and logic-reachable knowledge is also not new, we return to the shocking modern thoughts of the Greek philosophy, especially to the most important skeptics in Chapter 4 on uncertainty.

The uncertainty about the truth of any human judgment was reflected in the Platonic dialogs, the till now referenced origins of metaphysical thinking. The diversion remained rooted in beliefs about the existence about a metaphysical final truth, its definition and accessibility. The key for access was the instrument of partly benevolent, partly power-coveting people and organizations or in the resigned appearance of social-historical depression.

The novelty in logic and related scientific, computational progress was the experimental model realization through the instrument of highly advanced mathematics, physics, and philosophy of logic. The new models were definitely different from the earlier imaginative pictures of the world. They resulted in deep functional connections of observed phenomena and provable predictions about further factual manifestations of nature. This revolution started an even more general view of science disciplines, instead of strengthening the opposite world view of mystic metaphysical irrationalism.

The perfect-looking closed world of science formed a frontier between the scientifically reachable and the realm of metaphysically inaccessible. This frontier was consciously defined by the majority of philosophers and scientists, or was packed into another belief of rather shortly achievable human omnipotence. Paradoxically, the idea of human omnipotence emerged as another form of metaphysical beliefs. The abolition of the barriers of the unknown opened a higher freedom of scientific thinking and model building. The extensions of these limits can even be measured in the dimensions reached in the past century, to fentoseconds and billions of years, in nanometers to hundreds of millions of light-years. These esoteric-looking cosmological dimensions appear now in everyday practices of technology and biotechnology-based medicine.

The novelty of this rational openness could integrate the evolutionary relevance of knowledge based on scientific disciplines. A milestone of this new rationalist view was marked by the final-looking theological separation of science and theology by the *Fides et Ratio* Encyclical Letter of Pope John Paul II in 1998. The realms of numeric infinity, general relativity, and quantum phenomena are no longer territories of speculation but open, free fields for research progress with similar limitations regarding the present existence of the human race. Consequently, the investigations of the human social, historical, and psychological behavior remain in the realm of scientific research.

3.1.4. OPEN AND CLOSED CONCEPTUAL WORLDS

The concept of open, infinite worlds started a new epoch in the ways of thinking, influencing mathematics, physics, and social sciences. For us, it can be accepted with some historical empathy; why was this revolution so difficult to accept for the brightest minds of mankind? Support for understanding that weakness is a glance at the immense depth of unfolded uncertainty, dangers of metaphysical misrepresentations in algebra, as was discussed in Chapter 2.

The process of this rearrangement of thinking is, by definition, an infinite one. The relevant quality is the evolutionary, approximative character. This world view, being more and more abstracted and requiring more and more difficult conceptual, mathematical instrumentation, raises one of the most difficult problems of the modern age. The unfolding of firm frames puts mankind in a new individual and social responsibility position without the earlier virtual but strong working crutches and barriers.

The conceptual world of constructive skepticism has tried for some time to establish a modest guidance for this responsibility.

Computer science, as emphasized many times, tries to respond to the new understanding problem by its means. These means reflect the consciousness of artificial framings and support the approximation attempts in pragmatic tasks of technology and more subtle problems of human communication with and by machines.

The logical answer was the experiment with closing the world of discourse, definition of the validity limitations under the denomination: non-monotonic logic. *Circumscription, default logic, temporal, situation logic* covered the same effort as was brilliantly shown by the pioneer of that renewed way of local thinking (McCarthy, 2007). The crucial task was and still is the appropriate definition of the constraints which create a closed world of acceptable, relative truth. The difference in approach is essentially epistemic: instead of a hypothetical perfect world of logic, artificially closed realms are defined with the conscious knowledge of their imperfection and continuous check for improving these closures, a critical revision of omitted effects. This is the practical acknowledgement of the previous philosophical considerations about new freedoms, new responsibilities and actual limitations. In Appendix 3.2 a slightly more detailed explanation is given about non-monotonic logic.

Regarding limit definitions, the means are nothing but the regular expressive formulae of classic logic. The use of quantifiers and the inclusion of some uncertainty measures were given solutions. All further novelties—continuing the malicious remarks of our superficial critical observers—are nothing more than an abundant stream of not-too-creative publications, attempts at the popular renaming of existing concepts and methods.

On the less pragmatic side, the mathematical-philosophical discussion of the Pre-Gödelian period—until the early thirties of the 20th century—prepared a rich continuation of conceptual and formal clarifications, most of them we enjoy now in various results born from mother algebra.

The frontiers of the seizable and non-seizable were widened and in our current years experimental physics and material science has witnessed the realities, new seizabilities of this esoteric freedom and regularity of nature and nature-given practice. In physics, the non-existence of an absolute inertial system, of an absolute reference, and experimental results in quantum entanglement are good examples.

The new freedom of thinking, emerging at the turn to the 20th century, also provoked a fundamental philosophical rethinking of the nature of mathematics. In our context this should be mentioned, due to its epistemic relation to mathematics, reality, and the mind.

This new revolution started with Cantor, with his hardly understood ideas about different scales of infinity, embedded into more and more infinite classes. He really opened a world beyond the traditional common limits. The other, nearly contemporary breakthrough was the acceptance of geometries beyond the habitual, an axiomatic prolongation of the infinities in spaces. These were the Bolyai-Lobachewsky and Riemann geometries, esteemed and applied later, the fantasy-moving extension of the Euclidean view that was canonized for more than two thousand years.

To the preliminaries belonged the rethinking of natural-looking basic concepts, as the natural number by Peano, operations by Zermelo and Fraenkel, and later the new axiomatization of logic by Tarski and Post showed, as well as the encyclopedic approach of the French Bourbaki group. These names characterize a great progress within about a century. The best review of those interacting generations is given in a few recently republished reviews of the original publications (Hawking, 2005; Davis 1965). Their definitional rigor was reflected in the pertaining notational novelties and refinement. Most of these refinements reappeared in the type categorizations, ways of thinking in computer languages.

These partly metamathematical accomplishments give birth to latent questions: How were these accomplishments—and mathematics in general—born? Are they inherent with the creation of the world, closely connected to the divine order of the Game of Life in the universe? Or as a separate spiritual entity, created only by the human mind and free from any kind of further imaginations, preserving only its internal rules and own logical coherence? Another return of the Platonic problem! One of the relevant answers was the development of constructive, intuitionist mathematics. Constructive is the collective designation of the trend, and intuitionist is the best known and elaborated version, due especially to the activity of Brouwer.

The given freedom constitutes a challenge against the phrase "there exists…." Seeking to supplant it with the wording "we can construct…" The consequence can be a different kind of mathematics, due to Brouwer and others, and especially to the heavy criticism by the greatest contemporary mathematicians, a full-fledged, well constructed logic. The not-so-surprising result was a not-too-different construct!

From the epistemic point of view, the relevance of this mental attitude is twofold. First, it can generally open the thinking about similarities and differences of our abstracted ideas in relation to reality, as it was and is still the main line of modern theoretical physics. The second is a related new opening towards unconventional world views, being fundamentally different from earlier models.

An expansion of this idea is offered by von Neumann, in his talk "The Role of Mathematics in the Sciences and in Society" (Neumann, 1954), which is here quoted at length:

> There have been very serious fluctuations in the professional opinion of mathematicians on what mathematical rigor is. In my own experience, which extend over only some thirty years, it has fluctuated so considerably, that my personal and sincere conviction as to what mathematical rigor is, has changed at least twice. [...]
>
> Let me now speak further of the function of mathematics specifically in our thinking. It is commonplace that mathematics is an excellent school of thinking, that it conditions you to logical thinking, that after having experienced it you can somehow think more validly than otherwise. I don't know whether all these statements are true, the first one is probably least doubtful. However, I think it has a very great importance in thinking in an area which is not so precise. I feel that one of the most important contributions of mathematics to our thinking is, that it has demonstrated an enormous flexibility in the formation of concepts, a degree of flexibility to which it is very difficult to arrive in a non-mathematical mode. One sometimes finds somewhat similar situations in philosophy; but those areas of philosophy usually carry much less conviction.

The more detailed considerations about these mental and observational relations come back several times; moreover, in some sense, it is the main subject of our work: the reality, its infinite faces, its evolutionary reflections in the brain, the brain's construct in models, hypotheses, and theories. They create a continuum, a very long track, historically and mentally. The development can bring about any kind of deviation, useful in some period or malignant with respect to further progress or working. The recommended way is the kind of continuous feedback that is defined as *constructive skepticism*.

One of the best definitions of the method can be quoted from the economist Leontief:

True advance can be achieved only through an iterative process in which improved theoretical formulation raises new empirical questions and the answers to these questions, in their turn, lead to new theoretical insights. The "givens" of today become the "unknowns" that will have to be explained tomorrow this, incidentally, makes untenable the admittedly convenient methodological position according to which a theorist does not need to verify directly the factual assumptions on which he chooses to base his deductive arguments, provided his empirical conclusions seem to be correct. The prevalence of such a point of view is, to a large extent, responsible for the state of splendid isolation in which our discipline nowadays finds itself.

Other references to the multiuse wording of *constructive skepticism* and this book's attitudes will return in Chapter 5.

The attribute, *constructive*, in this epistemic context, has a meaning different from that in the concrete mathematical discipline. Nevertheless, they have some intrinsic relation in the view of the absolute *true* and in the approach of a better looking model. Some advocates of constructive mathematics claim that this different construct might have relevant roles in computer science and its resulting practice.

The epistemic relevance is emphasized here. It is somehow similar to the realization of the roundness of the world, of dimensions in distance, easier or hardly accessible regions, other ways of life and thinking, and the new consciousness of linguistic and power limits. The other, frequently quoted lesson was the posterior practical applicability. Cryptography, as mentioned, is only one example. The fast developing application of number-theoretical aspects of mathematics demonstrate many other examples: in search methods, problems relating to signal processing, design of economic, reliable, recoverable codes, data structuring and mining, and in problems of computational complexity. The Einsteinian-Riemannian world geometry and the quantum theory are now engineering instruments in power generation and material technology research.

The state of being open and simultaneously aware of being relatively closed in the infinite conceptual world is a special freedom, enjoyed only recently in our present model-driven world. Model driven is understood in factual computer models and more generally in the universe of scientific, rational considerations of any kind.

3.1.5. Some Possible Escape Exits from the Vague Future

A rather presumptuous hypothesis suggests that we really reached the end of that way. *That way* must be emphasized, similarly to the Gödelian revolution we can always accept the possibility of anything very alien from the habitual way. Two areas are currently present in the non-committed brains. The first is related to the entanglement phenomenon of quantum mechanics, the physical existence of the earlier, only hypothetical simultaneous twin states. The single qubit now is present in the experimentally repeatable quantum effect. The effort, for doing the same, in a reliable, computationally applicable way in evaluating earlier intractably complex phenomena, is a challenge for many devoted research groups. The present situation is agnostic; neither the possibility, nor the impossibility is proved.

Nevertheless, the mathematics of these qubit operations should not differ fundamentally from the usual means: operations of logic and some kinds of uncertainty, probability, statistical methods, of course, in some highly advanced and novel appearance. An impressive example is Shor's algorithm for factoring integers and Grover's method for much faster search. The idea is really remarkable, how a wide spectrum of knowledge can generate novelties from the earlier, often mutually unrelated ideas. The number-theoretical, algebraic

Houses from factors and the residuum modules

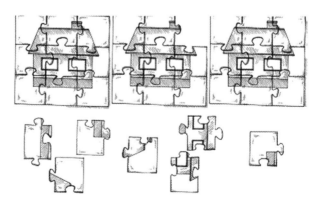

concept of *factors* provides a possibility for narrowing the range of the unknown to closer territories. The *factors*, like the prime factors of an integer or the root factors of an equation or differential equation, indicate the similarities, homologies within groups. The *residuums* mark the difference, sometimes the distance from the group and refer to other ideas of problem solving, now after factorization, in a more stripped, simplified manner. The residuums, like our figure about prefab houses, made of factorizable components, reflect the problem of composition and the possibility of resolving the task. The *modulo calculation* opens some new opportunities in handling a much smaller and limited range of items. With some generalization, this is an analogous route of many research attempts.

The other hypothetical thought-experiment is even more remote. Quantum logic should apply results of quantum theory, the other idea is a thought experiment in the world of general relativity, permitting different relations in different worlds of different velocities and gravitational circumstances (Andréka et al., 2006).

3.2. Logic in Computers

Da wird der Geist euch wohl dressiert / In spanische Stiefeln eingeschnürt / Daß er bedächtiger so fort an / Hinschleiche die Gedankenbahn / Und nicht etwa, die Kreuz und Quer / Irrlichteliere hin und her. / Dann lehret man euch manchen Tag / Daß, was Ihr sonst auf Einen Schlag / Getrieben, wie Essen und Trinken frei / Eins! Zwei! Drei! dazu nöthig sei. / Zwar ists mit der Gedankenfabrik / Wie mit einem Webermeisterstück / Wo Ein Tritt tausend Fäden regt / Die Schifflein herüber hinüber schießen / Die Fäden ungesehen fließen / Ein Schlag tausend Verbindungen schlägt. / Der Philosoph, der tritt herein / Und beweist Euch, es müßt so sein: / Das Erst wär so, das Zweite so / Und drum das Dritt und Vierte so; / Und wenn das Erst und Zweit nicht wär / Das Dritt und Viert wär nimmermehr. Das preisen die Schüler allerorten / Sind aber keine Weber geworden. / Wer will was Lebendigs erkennen und beschreiben / Sucht erst den Geist heraus zu treiben / Dann hat er die Theile in seiner Hand.

(Then will your mind be so well braced / In Spanish boots so tightly laced /That on 'twill circumspectly creep / Thought's beaten track securely keep / Nor will it, ignis-fatuus like / Into the path of error strike. / Then

many a day they'll teach you how/ The mind's spontaneous acts, till now/ As eating and as drinking free /Require a process—one! two! three!/ In truth the subtle web of thought / Is like the weaver's fabric wrought: / One treadle moves a thousand lines / Swift dart the shuttles to and fro / Unseen the threads together flow / A thousand knots one stroke combines./ Then forward steps your sage to show / And prove to you, it must be so;/ The first being so, and so the second / The third and fourth deduc'd we see; / And if there were no first and second / Nor third nor fourth would ever be. / This, scholars of all countries prize—/ Yet 'mong themselves no weavers rise— / He who would know and treat of aught alive, / Seeks first the living spirit thence to drive: / Then are the lifeless fragments in his hand

Johann Wolfgang von Goethe, *Faust*

3.2.1. DUBIOUS CONTRIBUTION OF NON-MONOTONIC LOGIC

Under the pressure of all rational problems, several attempts, non-monotonic methods as well as typical methods, try to go around the binary limit of the ideal *true-false* (and therefore *else*…) trap, related to the closed world assumption. That is not a ternary system in the regular sense, because the ternary, in the closed worlds, can be resolved by two binaries, both pointing to certain definite points inside the closed world borders or to the infinite areas of the open world. This does not provide definite answers, only occasionally, and give some indications about the nature of that unknown world. Existence, in a limited probabilistic, uncertainty field, such as early maps showing undiscovered territories:

The escape ways are recursive in their theoretical limitations—they return to the classic discipline. The problem is treated more intrinsically later in this chapter.

The opening of many simultaneous worlds means either the handling of many simultaneous closed worlds or the simultaneous handling of closed worlds and of open ones, characterized by some uncertainty-type features and uncertain boundaries, i.e., results on a higher level but of the same nature. The search methods of the practical and also of the research-oriented mind apply this simultaneous frame scheme; all current discoveries about the brain activity suggest the hypothetical model.

Hic sunt dracones (here are dragons).

The real methodological answers lie, most probably, in the application of other disciplines, about semantics of the knowledge field and in some pragmatic approximations, i.e., beyond any direct mathematical-logical methods.

3.2.2. Complex Problem Solving

The novelty is now a healthy pragmatic trend for solving the computational problems of real life systems of real complexity. This novelty has a much more profound relevance than any highly practical software. The computer analysis of a complex structure supports the discovery of the essential structure of the subject one hidden in the bypasses, the non-direct ways of thinking, and the memory-based patterns of earlier ideas. The search for optimal logical structures is a part of data mining for the structural skeleton of the subject. Several problem-oriented software systems follow this line. Service-oriented structures are popular examples. The practical approach hides a certain preconception about the model structure and the difficulties of standardization versus flexibility. The results are therefore contradictory: We treat a big system with much effort for individual applications or problem-oriented schemes, which are hardly capable of innovation. The compromises require double faculties of a wide and deep experience based on knowledge and a practical expertise weighing ad hoc possibilities. This essay can contribute in only a very limited way to the first and nothing to the second.

The role of the structural skeleton should be revisited here in relation to the most ambitious logic-based program, the PROLOG in Appendix 3.4.

Our purpose is to show the power of notation and the limits of logic, i.e., the ubiquity of Greek syllogistics and the strength of the further abstractions by notation.

Several further structural programming simplifications–creating hierarchies of statements about truth or false consequences, naming, and defining further abstractions–can be added to consolidate certain knowledge. The knowledge itself stands beyond and not in the logic programming, and that is the main lesson for us, the window for limits of knowledge.

The most important and possibly misleading limit is the nature of truth and the indefinite or definite limits of statements relative to the changing and uncertain environment of any real milieu.

Logic programming and other logic-based knowledge-related systems can be used for a practical dialog system of knowledge acquisition if the questioning agent knows what to ask a question about and the answerer knows the answer, i.e., if the partners can be unified logically to complete a closed field of knowledge where the closure is completed by the *don't know* expression.

Such is the case in the usual expert systems' design, a practical but misleading one if the case is not as simple as most user manuals, or as sophisticated and sincere to apply the *don't know* term rather frequently. Otherwise, it is not more than a well prepared questionnaire of any administration, with definite interrogative pronouns. The inclusion of indefinite interrogatives requires external knowledge.

These systems are very useful for reference to man-machine systems and to the role of the human partner in man–machine symbiosis. Speaking more generally, if adequate definitions are available for a linguistic subject, i.e., all objects, actions, and qualifiers are accepted for a discourse concerned, everything can be expressed and communicated by means of logic. This could be proved even for poetic sentiments–of course if these sentiments have adequate definitions–or for any esoteric theory of science. A full, logic representation of the theory of general relativity has been completed just recently (Szabó, 2008).

The grounding of logic in human experience is the classic Wittgensteinian standpoint referred to in the *Tractatus*–the final conclusion on what cannot be expressed and the problem of the Faustian motto.

Software systems design or support the design of query and concept-definition languages. Their problem is the same when speaking about system structures. The two are closely related. A good traditional interrogator could penetrate into the elucidation task, using previous experience and getting free of obvious prejudices.

The limit looks to be the same as that of language, but this is not enough! Each word, each expression has deep and practically infinite background relations in individual history, social and other momentary and past situations, in the relation of the issuer and the recipient. This immense background is present also during the whole history of remote communication access, started with the ever renewed stories of ancient rhapsodists. The highbrow problem of these relativities has been interesting for philosophers, aestheticians, and historians until now, as we put the majority of communication in computers, frequently without the considerations of necessary human relations. Communication with call centers and administrative questionnaires are irksome and comic examples.

3.2.3. Logic and Paradoxes, Undecidability

Ill-stated systems and their logic-conducted search frequently end in paradoxes. The problem of paradoxes has irritated logicians through the centuries and stimulated novel solutions within the frame of logic, less within the softer conceptual world of linguistics. The paradoxical limits of logical reasoning were nice philosophical and linguistic games. Now, logic being the essential instrument of reasoning via computers, leaks of logic can cause erroneous results, possibly catastrophes. These leaks are particularly related to the limitations of conceptual definitions. The paradoxes of Appendix 3.7 are entertaining ancient examples.

A relevant remark should be added to the uncertainties and volatile nature of definitions—the Gödelian limitation of completeness in sufficiently complex definitional systems as a final result of the great efforts outlined here in very simplified interpretations.

Gödel stated, in a very modest remark about his achievement:

> … there is also a close relationship with the Liar Paradox… Every epistemological antinomy can be used for a similar proof of undecidability.
>
> Before we go into details, let us first sketch the main ideas of the proof, naturally without making any claim to rigor. The formulas of a formal system (we limit ourselves here to the system PM) are, considered from the outside, finite sequences of primitive symbols (variables, logical constants, and parentheses or dots) and one can easily make completely precise which sequences of primitive symbols are meaningful formulas and which are not. Analogously, from the formal standpoint, proofs are nothing but finite sequences of formulas (with certain specifiable properties). Naturally, for metamathematical considerations, it makes no difference which objects one takes as primitive symbols, and we decide to use natural numbers for that purpose. Accordingly, a formula is a finite sequence of natural numbers and a proof-figure is a finite sequence of finite sequences of natural numbers. Metamathematical concepts (assertions) thereby become concepts (assertions) about natural numbers or sequences of such, and therefore (at least partially) expressible in the symbolism of the system PM itself.

These are Gödel's explanations in his seminal work *On Formally Undecidable Propositions of Principia Mathematica and Related Systems*. *PM* in the above quotation is a reference to the *Principia Mathematica* of Russell and Whitehead.

The revolutionary novelty lies in the perception and proof of a much more general and pervasive reality of logic. All cited paradoxes are epistemic, i.e., their contradictive content follows from the understanding of the given situation; the interpretation of the content clarifies the gist.

3.2.4. ABOUT THE GÖDELIAN EPISTEMIC

Gödel discovered something very different: independent of the subject, from the very contents, in well designed logical systems a paradoxical situation is possible, the deduced result of the axioms, for example the initial statements can not prove the correctness of the initials nor of the results. The relativity of this procedure of truth search is a consequence of the infinity of worlds, world situations, and the related problem of definitions for closed parts of these worlds. These definitions are the axioms of the system, described by the theoretical instruments of logic.

These types of considerations were alien for the best minds of the late 19th century in their renewed endeavor for coronation of the second phase of the enlightenment. The program, best conceived in the *Principia* of Russell and Whitehead, was to create a theoretically consistent and logical (both mathematical and philosophical) super-tower of all sciences. This was conformant with the farsighted *Hilbertian program*, too. The perspective was a logically uniform explanation and description of nature with a hope of getting instruments for the reconstructing of everything available in the cognicized world.

The first great hit on this eternal human idea was the Cantorian theory of infinity and infinities of different embedded complexity classes.

Gödel's proof was accepted relatively fast and its power helped science open its view on unconsolidated hypotheses and theories about the physical, biological, and social nature, i.e., not abandoning the continuous developmental view and activity of science, but broadening its theoretical visual angle. The practical result is the epistemic view of modern computer-built theoretical and engineering creations, in this book's sense, in *creative skepticism*.

Coming back to the Gödelian proof, the ingenuity and relevance lies in the raising of the paradox from its epistemic content. That is the reason for the use of the clumsy looking but fantastically witty Gödelian numbering. Using numbers, i.e., of the same general abstracted coordinates (*remember the ideas about algebra*), for symbols of arithmetic operations and unification of these with the coordinate numerals that can symbolize anything of the factual items. On the one hand, Gödel received logical sentences and deduction operations of the simplest natural-number representation, and on the other, in the most general expressions.

An important remark about the continuity of thinking and acceptance: The way how Gödel developed his proof was prepared by Löwenheim in 1915. According to his theorem, a scheme provable in the domain of natural numbers, or in any countable infinite domain, is valid universally. Natural numbers represent a fundamental scheme of ordered items. If some axiomatic relations are attached to this order, it should be valid for the whole uniformly ordered scheme. This theorem and the further works of Skolem helped not only Gödel in his thinking but also prepared the experienced minds for reception. In these processes of pioneering and reception sometimes the direct contact is not the relevant motivation but the atmosphere of creative communities. From this point of view several priority quarrels look to be irrelevant.

An earlier experiment in numbering mathematical definitions about positive integer numbers and looking for paradoxical behavior was initiated by the French mathematician Richard in 1905. The paradox was resolved by its definitional deficiency, the example of Richard's paradox and its relevance in this trend, proves only the usually necessary atmosphere for a new milestone in the history of thought and scholarly understanding.

Gödel expressed the sets of a generally valid, true statements and of their negations. He proved that two contradictory expressions or sentences can lead to an ambiguous conclusion, just like the *Cretan case* or other paradoxes show, but now the two initial statements say only that this statement is true or false. The recursive sequence of the Gödelian proof procedure says that generally, and regardless of content, "in definite logical systems there are formulae (statements), which are true but not provable within the definite system, not reducible to the initial proof formulae."

The Gödel number expressions, in the role of any concrete verbal logical sentence, are now the highest distilled forms of any formal system. These formal systems are based on axioms and premissae, expressed in the mathematical–computational models. An easy proof for the reader could be a transcript of a PROLOG program in the Gödelian notation.

The original papers and an abundance of excellent, theoretically correct and pedagogically lucid literature can conduct the interested and prepared reader through this beautiful alley of mathematical logic (Hofstadter, 1979; Smullyan, 1992 etc.). Still more reference, some correct, some superficial, can be found about the resulting theses. The purpose of this recital was a demonstration of the development of an ancient playful problem to a decisive, revolutionary general view about the limits of logical thinking, and of the admirable power of mathematical logic, abstracted thinking in the critical thinking about itself.

The Gödelian revolution leads further to the problems of the artificially and practically closed world borders. In Russell's discussion the Cantorian problem was defined by the question: is the border, the conceptual entity, a part of the entity or not? (Appendix 3.5) In computer science the reference is the program. The computational *halting problem* of *Turing* is not only a theoretical but a practical example. According to the problem definition, if we have a program and a final input, how can it be decided that the program finishes running or continues forever? The initial conditions of the program cannot define in general if the program doesn't run into a circular loop.

The practical problems, of the artificial closing the naturally infinite or practically not computable worlds of modeling, are main subjects of uncertainty. They are treated in the next chapter. Chaitin gives a nice definition of randomness deduced from the Gödelian incompleteness concepts: "Although randomness can be precisely defined and can even be measured, a given number cannot be proved to be random. This enigma establishes a limit to what is possible in mathematics" (Chaitin, 2006).

In this respect we have to refer to the development of the number concept and the even more general difference between reality and its mathematical model. Randomness of a number is a connotative quality, a reference to the generation mode of the number, e.g., dicing or computational generation of pseudorandom numbers. Accordingly, the Kolmogorov definition is similar: "Random is a number which cannot be generated by a shorter program than the notation of the number within the same numbering system."

Random phenomena have random metric in their temporal or other physical occurrence relations. Between two first prizes in lottery the time interval is random. These can be taken or not taken to be enigmatic or mystical only in the subjective view of the observer person.

This incompleteness is detectable not only in the original strong mathematical environment of theorems and proofs but in any conversation, too, each having some kind of circularities, self-references. These now obvious circumstances and caveats don't wreck the results of science achieved and proven till now but put only into a cautiously skeptic light to preserve or to improve the earlier and new constructions.

In these perspectives the original Russellian-Hilbertian program does not lose its value—it is even stronger working in the attempts to investigate the frontiers and coherences of the currently accessible world knowledge, emphasizing the open nature of all these limitations and links.

3.2.5. The Semantic Question

The syntactic features of logic programming permit and even support the creation of semantic definitions, as it was detailed more in this chapter earlier. Usually, the problem is therefore hidden in the uncertain truth values of their definitions and logic consequences, i.e., in the epistemic problem of related knowledge. The same is even more valid for any kind of non-monotonic logic where the limitations of validity are given in similar definition terms, should they be temporal, situational limits or limits expressed by the definition of default values. This can be considered a general aspect of the theoretical looking-halting problem: how can a program be certain about its own semantic limitations?

The introduction of soft truth was a logical step after having accepted the skeptic views about the fragile nature of truth. That line of soft logic started in a rather indirect way at the end of the 19th century with thinking about subjective probability and reached its proliferation with fuzzy logic and psychology-based estimations. We come back to these developments in the next chapter about uncertainty, to the subject as the best indicator of epistemic relations.

A relevant addition to logic theory is the strong classifications of different kinds of logic—propositional, first-order, orders of further arity, classical and non-classical, formal definitions of proofs, and validity—all based on the theoretical developments.

These definitions are available in many recent textbooks, and they essentially help in a critical view of any highly complex algorithmic procedure. The applied proof methods of the truth value of some propositions depend on the applicability of the procedure for the art of logic used in the computational process.

3.2.6. Modalities, Intensions, Algebraic Structures of Logic

All basic contradictions of logic to be used as a final instrument (for theology i.e., divine origins) of proving truth, were rather clear for the founding fathers of logic, i.e., for the thinkers of Antiquity. Just because of that importance, related to the problem of truth in general, and the final truth incorporated in the different beliefs of divine origin, the subject was and is still a focus of human thinking. To illustrate how old the realization of these problems were, read Kallimachos, the great librarian of Alexandria, who wrote in the third century BCE in an epigram: "Even the crows on the roofs caw about the nature of conditionals" (cited by Kneale and Kneale, 1971).

The inclusion of modalities, i.e., of conditionals related to environmental, personal and temporal conditions, was a subject of continuous development during the Middle Ages and in so-called modern logic. This concluded in much, now superficial-looking, obstinacy but also in a continuous refinement of thinking about the *de dicto – de re* (of what is said, of the thing). It is more and more a current problem of communication. By the relevance of the third constituent, the intermediate communication channel and its social-technological complex we feel difficulties fast increasing. Linguistic divergence of concepts, feelings, beliefs, intentions change after being issued and are distorted from the very instant of the mental representation till the acceptance of the message.

The refinement resulted in a deep understanding of these ternary relations, those of the issuer, the medium, and the receiver. Above the subjective existence of that trinity work the relations of the original phenomena and of the resulting actions. This is now a basic and thus far unsolved problem of a global, medium-representational human society. The conceptual means of modern logic–the concepts of complexity, computability, infinity, different conceptual worlds, limits of completeness in axiomatic-theoretical reasoning–clarified the impossibility of any final solution. The reality-oriented, rationally thinking people were inspired to find feasible compromises and to accept the temporal, environmental, individual nature of communication and control. Here, we met another relevant epistemic lesson.

These mind-sharpening refinements, the developments of modal logic, distinctions of more objective-looking extensions of propositions and intension-related sentences, led to more subjective modalities.

A modern continuation of the Middle Ages considerations about the *de dicto* - *de re* problem i.e., the separation of the information from its real subject, were the developments of Barcan Marcus and Kripke with definitions of the modalities related to different worlds. These different worlds are subject and temporal bounds that continuously change the mental world and consequent responses, as no two persons have the exact same views on anything factual in their own.

All these developments, ideas and methods are wonderfully explained in an endless multitude of literature on historical evolution, mathematical and philosophical details, and computational know-how. The literature covers every level of educational background from the primary school to the highest scholarly requirements. The purpose of this chapter is restricted to lessons for our current epistemic conclusions.

Logic, in the mirror of information technology and, therefore, in epistemic considerations, developed from a beautiful and sometimes bloody exercise of thinking and debates, mixed with ideologies and power intentions. Now, it can be used, hopefully, rather as a discipline and practice of everyday computation, equipped with all the great results and onerous responsibilities of our everyday life. Another face of *constructive skepticism*!

In this context two conclusions should be emphasized: the first is the fact of a final reduction of all sophisticated logical instruments to the classic first-order logic, in a sense that it can describe computations completely; the second are the consequences of the not transparent complexity of all highly intricate computational procedures which have their origins in the elaborate structures built of these primitives.

In spite of all these refinements and extensions, the basic epistemic lesson remains valid: all extensions can be interpreted in the historically oldest and most simple formulae of propositional logic. What is even more important, for the purposes of computation, this simplification and interpretation should be done, though now these are hidden in the automatic procedures of logic programming based methods. Every further doubt is shifted towards linguistics, as Kolmogorov (1925) asserts in his considerations about the *pseudotruth* and *pseudomathematics,* we can add psychology, social sciences, and arts. These all were rather clear for the open minds, the essential novelty is their packaged, hidden presence and relevant roles in all the three phases of communication software, as a new actor beyond and within the issuer and the receiver.

3.2.7. CIRCULARITY: DANGERS AND ROLES

The phenomenon of the circularity danger must be mentioned here, too. Virtual bases for complex logical structures are the definition procedures of logic statements. These virtual bases are the explanations of the name primitives and further the definitions of limitations. These node-like virtual bases of complex logical structures are mostly expressed by variables. The variables represent the validity ranges and truth values of complex constructs. Unfortunately, these cannot be regularly surveyed, nor can the argumentations, decisions, and material constructs. The results of the correct logical procedures serve as affirmatives for the initial definitions. This recurrent false circle is not exceptional but usual. The results appear in mistakes or even misdeeds in any professional looking procedures, leading to fatal consequences and justifications thereof.

All kinds of statements based on some ideological, power-related legal definitions, all hypothetical development lines of science, preserved erroneously for a long time, are instructive examples. Linguistic definitions, especially not well-proven etymologies, belong to this class.

Circularity

On the other hand, this circularity, applied as feedback for definitional hypotheses, is the only recommendable way for hypothesis enforcement. Enforcement is a cautious definition, too, leading to seemingly final problems of epistemic truth, validity, and falsification. In several cases that feedback-validation procedure cannot be accepted either as final decisions in any critical case nor as final refutations of a hypothesis, in the Popperian sense. In the next chapter on uncertainty, we return to relevant circularities in our usual scientific observation theory feedback and data mining practice.

The Popperian requirement was the combination of proof for a theory with the possibility of a proof of its negation. In our computer epistemology, this leads to the resolution programming applied in PROLOG, too. The idea goes back to the *reductio ad absurdum* (reduction to the contradictory absurdity of the opposite statement) method of ancient logic (Popper, 1935, 1959, 1963).

All these are well acceptable with the closed (and completely revealable) world hypotheses or hypothetical search attempts within uncertain conceptual worlds. In this sense, Lakatos defined his *research program* ideas much closer to the above considerations about models for representation (Lakatos, 1976).

In computational practice, we meet circularity in infinite loops of programs; states which do not lead to any kind of result.

3.3. ABOUT FINAL TRUTH, EPISTEMIC ETHICS

What makes all doctrines plain and clear?
About two hundred pounds a year.
And that which was proved true before,
Prove false again? Two hundred more.
Butler, *Hudibras*, III./1277

The problem of any final truth can only be reduced to the individual death of an individual and, even in this subject, biology has some slightly uncertain answers related to the decision point of letting a body follow its natural decay. The remark concerning the proverbial human lethal case: nothing is certain but death (and taxes) is not an emphasis on triviality. What is final can only be individual for individuals, considering our current final epistemic horizon. Not more and not less, every other epistemic and epistemically consequent problem is open, infinite for other individuals, especially for the coming generations and for the encounters of those generations with the infinity of natural phenomena. Quoting Wittgenstein: "The world and life are one," (5.621) and "I am my world. (The microcosm.)" (5.63).

The logic of limits of logic and the epistemic consideration about those limitations of the infinity horizon is a rather new starting point of ethics. This means the responsibility of the individual limits and freedom dimensions of responsibility are the deepest and most relevant conundrum of mankind, from the very start of thinking about ourselves and nature.

The valuation of any result rendered by computer-assisted logic should be the subject of this constructive epistemic-ethical responsibility.

Final end ?

CHAPTER 4

How Uncertain is Uncertainty?

Solum certum nihil esse certi
Nothing is certain but uncertainty
Pliny, the elder, *Historia Naturalis*

4.1. A Long Story of Uncertainty about Uncertainty

4.1.1. THEY HAVE NO SCIENCE?

We are unable to get deep into the minds of our ancestors. Nevertheless, we can draw some hypotheses on their beliefs, on their view about the world order, mirrored in their fantasy. With some certainty, we can state that most of the events and circumstances were uncertain for them, especially from our point of view. The difference in definition is relevant for the whole essay. What I take as certain, can be uncertain for any contemporary and even more for somebody living in the future and possessing much deeper knowledge about the phenomena.

Fuzzy end

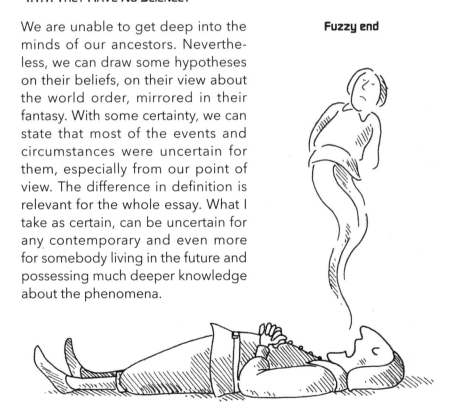

Horrors of the past and present

The world was almost totally uncertain for those who had to transfer all causes to imagined beings.

Centuries of rites and traditions of transition and continuation have rendered even the most certain event, death, ambiguous. That primitive looking manner of burial cults survives still in more sublime forms of current highbrow civilizations.

Tales, sculptural figures, and preserved folklore all testify the hypothesis that ancient man, due to a general feeling of uncertainty—exposed to fire, wars, famine, epidemics, disasters of natural environment—was much more hysteric than the everyman of today.

Continuity and change can be perceived by a quotation from the silver age of Antiquity, about 200 CE, written by one of the Fathers of the Church, Tertullian:

> If you look at the world as a whole, you cannot doubt that it has grown progressively more cultivated and populated. Every territory is now accessible, every territory explored, every territory opened to commerce, the most delightful farmsteads have obliterated areas formerly waste, plough-land has subdued the woods, domestic cattle have put to flight the wild beast, barren sands have become fertile, rocks are reduced to soil, swamps are drained, the number of cities today's exceeds the number of isolated huts in former times, islands no longer inspire fear nor crags terror: everywhere people, everywhere organized communities, everywhere human life. Most convincing as evidence of populousness, we men have actually become a burden to the Earth, the fruits of nature hardly suffice to sustain us, there is a general pressure of scarcity giving rise to complaints, since the Earth can no longer support us. Need we be astonished that plague and famine, warfare and earthquake come to be regarded as remedies, serving as it were to trim and prune the superfluity of population?
>
> *(quoted by Cochrane, 1942)*

This mixture of mysticism and observation was true through the Middle Ages; Huizinga (1937) described it with lively documentation.

The divorce of uncertainty and certainty started with science. Science, *interpreted in our sense*, with reference to the Greek enlightenment, as it was interpreted in the first chapter. Generally speaking, until the high period of the Greek philosophy, people of the Mediterranean and Eastern civilizations observed plenty of remarkable phenomena and tried to register them in some order. A few of these observations can be considered of scientific character still in our eyes, but these people regarded the phenomenological facts as naturally given realities (all kind of spirits and gods included) and had no curiosity to search for further causes, interactions, generalizations, especially not in the frames of an organized, culturally adopted and critical search discipline.

This means, for the advanced Greeks, what could be included into the frame of their contemporary science was structured and disciplined in a new edifice of science; and all the rest formed the uncertain realm of non-science—beliefs, religions, curiosities. In that evolving rationalism, combined with the mythical foggy environment of the Pythagorean age, not even science and arts were separated. According to a witty remark of Russell, Pythagoras could have been some kind of a mixture of Einstein and Mary Eddy Baker, the 19th century founder of Christian Science.

We should add Schönberg, who constructed phonetic harmonies based on his mathematical-physical studies but added conscious and unconscious creativity in composing affectionate music. The problem of creating in a professional scientific method of the age concerned and the origins of surprising innate-looking creativity returns in the hypotheses about inherited, evolutionarily embedded interplays of these hidden structures and arising problems. Their associations and the mechanisms of these associations were long time problems of thinking about thinking. This was the subject in the second chapter about hypothetically hidden brain structures, in a related but slightly different context. Due to fast development of brain research we now have hope to approach these secrets in less vague ways.

Aristotle, in his unique effort in creating a rational, causal conceptual world, adhering to the sensible and conceivable world of the observable, separated the basic, causal and eternal looking primitives from the secondary, accidental features of these. He tried to do this separation with a reference to the accidental co-occurrence of the causal.

That view is still surviving in the philosophy of strong causality, though what we consider to be causal now, after experimental demonstration of the quantum physical entanglement, is even more open than it was for the geniuses of the last two and a half millennia. (Haenni, 2006.) The discussion of the current state of causal, accidental and other intermediate philosophical considerations lies much beyond the extent of this book.

We can only admire the pioneers of scientific thinking, and thinking in general, who tried to understand the world, first without prejudices and furthermore without any of the fantastic experimental observation devices of modern ages. The Aristotelian analysis of the accidental, secondary-looking features conclude in a definition very close to our information-theory view about signal and noise: "We have stated, then, what the accidental is, and from what cause it arises, and that there is no science which deals with it." (*Metaphysica*, E-2, 1027a, 26–27, Trans: W.D. Ross.)

The inclusion of these phenomena into the scope of science, as we understand it now, is a rather recent advance. Modeling of human behavior in economy and social sciences became now possible subjects of computational efforts. These models, at the time being, are demonstrations of the possibility to depict the phenomena by means of mathematics and by that to support the completing of more overall models. The results have, still now, stronger predictive and explicative power than the previous descriptive considerations. Nevertheless, the hard work in data mining and other modeling instrumentations, with more efforts in the socio-psychological research, promises relevant progress in this extremely important problem of human coexistence. From the point of view of rational and accidental frontiers, this can be a new milestone in epistemic progress. (Remember the quotation from Tertullian). The question is, can economic-social crisis be treated at last and pushed into the archives of history, like that of the plague?

Aristotle was "only" a beginning of modern scientific thinking but a long row of Greek philosophers added still remarkable thoughts to that beginning. Further some of the Greek thinkers started to contradict the rather fundamentalist looking causal-logical teaching of Aristotle. In the next chapter we return to up-to-date implications. The dogma of the *excluded middle* was and remained the cornerstone of that way of thinking and changed in the 20th century only as it was described in the third chapter, concerning open and closed worlds. Yes or no, true or false is always a pragmatic, sometimes necessary simplification of problems, though the reality covers the whole space between the two.

In this context it is rather difficult to reinterpret Aristotle's way of thinking and the ways of thinking of his followers who have written, preserved, and interpreted the dictum of the master. In *Metaphysica* (the name of Aristotle's philosophical writings that was given only later) the concept of *aporia* (puzzle, difficult open problem) could cover some of the fuzzy concepts, too.

4.1.2. THE SKEPTICS—FORERUNNERS OF MODERN SCIENCE PHILOSOPHY

From the partly lost, though still admirable, and still admirably rich treasury of Greek philosophy, I give prominence to the Skeptics. The unclear origins go back to the fourth or third century BCE, to Pyrrhon, and continuing under heavy criticism and several later additions to the texts of *Sextus Empiricus* and *Diogenes Laertios*, in the third century CE reporting especially on the modalities of Ainesidemos, who lived in the first century BCE.

In these modalities, the *tropos*, are collected ten various types of relativities in the perception of the reality. Most of these relativity modalities are parts of our commonsense thinking, are strikingly modern in our eyes, and provoked well understandable resistance on behalf of the most lucid contemporary Greek minds.

Due to the comparatively unknown skeptical heritage, and the relevance from our present points of view and arguments, the full text of the *tropos* definitions is added in Appendix 4.1.

The difficulties which the Skeptics suggest, relating to the agreement subsisting between what *appears to the senses, and what is comprehended by the intellect*, divide themselves into ten modes of argument, according to which the subject and object of our knowledge are essentially changing.

We can recognize rather precise definitions of modern ideas about the relativity of scientific concepts due to social conditions, i.e., the ideas of *Bloor* and the school of the social-philosophical "strong program." (See the fifth tropos in Appendix 4.1.) Even more interesting is the tropos about fuzzy nature or estimations, detailed in most of the modalities, regarding the estimation of the different agents, subjective and objective, environmental and sensory circumstances. These are really not different from the current fuzzy concept of Zadeh.

The world of uncertainty was alien for the rational, science-oriented philosophy that tried to include all phenomena into well-understandable and sensible general frames. They had to argue without the instruments of later periods that could establish differences much better, based on more sophisticated theories about causal relations.

4.1.3. NOMINALISTS OF MIDDLE AGES: DE DICTO – DE RE UNCERTAINTY

The philosophy of the Middle Ages, referring to several ideas of the Greek philosophy, concentrated on the divinely organized, overall regulated world view, was rationalist in that frame of belief. I have to emphasize that rational logic without the spirit of skepticism is always fragile, due to undiscovered phenomena and new, more powerful relational hypotheses. The quality of such beliefs can be measured on their epistemic power, how they work in different conditions, relations and how are they flexible for skeptical attitudes.

A remarkable historical example can be cited in order to explain the development of thinking in the Middle Ages. The canonized belief offered an overall explanation of everything and undertook to construct a classic, mostly corrupted, Aristotelian logic comprising all; but the same divine, not understandable, surprising wonders of everyday life generated more mysticism about the phenomena, relations that the contemporary discourse of science did not comprehend.

For us, the most relevant stream of thinking is the emergence of *nominalism*, the separation of the name from the named, *de dicto - de re* connection and antithesis. About the course of developments in thinking about logic, Kneale and Kneale (1962) illustrated an excellent review.

That line of thinking is one of the most important research areas of communication—the problem of adequate information emission and its perception. We can trace some past characteristics of the vehicle of information history by quoting the destiny of scripts and books. "Pro captu lectoris habent sua fata libelli," the booklets have their own fate, "how they are accepted by the reader," wrote Terentianus Maurus a grammatologist in the second century CE.

By the ubiquity and instant nature of the electronic information world, these questions received a highly practical relevance. One of these aspects is the indirect, *electronic representation of the individual, of the Self, used for all kinds of substitutions for the direct presence.* Personal identification is a crucial subject of individual freedom, privacy, and security.

The same, relativistic nominalist problem arises in the effects of various mass media, unprecedented manipulation technologies by electronic communication. The problem of legal regulation is now an everyday and ubiquitous scruple, depending on the supposed weights of communication perception of the population concerned.

The original problem was the representation of the *Script*, the two *Testaments* and later of the *Qur'an*, the contemporary and lin-guistical meanings of words, sentences and parables and the right and authority of interpretation as the second phase of the *de dicto – de re* representation process. The third, the problem of the claim for individual understanding, emerged within the discussions of the Reformation. Not by chance, the story was accelerando repeated in the tragicomic period of the original socialist ideas. The historical ref-erences indicate the cardinality of the problem, not less, but may be, even more and more explicitly present in the age of overall interme-diate, model-based, electronic telerepresentation.

The term *model-based* requires some explication. The best ex-amples are the personal questionnaires, especially those prepared by some administrative offices. They create personal models (profile models) of individuals and individual groups. These models can be good or bad, composed on the basis of long-term experience, even on valid legislative procedures; nevertheless, they reflect not only the requirements of the case but also a rather complete model of the person involved. The respondent should compress him/herself into this frame, imagine hypotheses about the aims of the questioner, in several cases having access only to the terms prepared by the office. You can think about the silly cases of tax formulae or visa applications.

We can return to the Aristotelian dictum—*has no science*—with the relevant complement: has no *unified* science. Further, we might add a disputable, not provable remark: will not have a unified science. Unified science is addressed, in spite of their theoretically provable incompleteness and continuous developments, moreover reinter-pretations, in ways dissimilar to other branches of mathematics.

4.1.4. MYSTIC OF UNCERTAINTY, MYSTIC OF LIFE: THE EARLY MESSAGE FROM INDIA

Uncertainty starts to be non-existing if it can be modeled in the way and reliability of scientific certainty. That is the reason why we cannot speak about uncertainty in general, as a subject of science and not as a concept of philosophy and general discourse.

Nala and Kali

This mystic of uncertainty could be one of the reasons why European science alienated itself from these irrational looking problems. Mathematics in India was put in a different framework, maybe due to the more natural attitude to nature. That was first admired by Europeans in respect of love, after this continent started to liberate itself from the ideological shackles, in the fresh air of the Renaissance and of the Age of Reason. One of the most famous love stories about a success, related to statistical estimation, was the tale of *Nala and Kali* (the latter was also a demigod of dancing). Nala could give a perfect estimation about the number of leaves and fruits on a big tree by calculating the relations between two typical singular branches and of the whole.

The original story was more ancient than the version referred to last, from about 400 CE. One of the more original texts of the Mahabharata (Book 3, Section LXXII) reports other versions and combines it with the father of dicing, Rituparna. Nevertheless, it is a mythological heritage about the origins of mathematical knowledge in high, mystical values.

4.1.5. WHERE SCIENCE STARTS AND SOPHISTICATED OBSERVATION ENDS

The other story from a rich civilization is the Persian fairy tale about *The three princes of Serendip* (Sri Lanka).

The narrative is a metaphor of making fortunate and unexpected discoveries by accident.

Horace Walpole made the story popular, but the beautiful origins and witty metaphors are best in the original tales, and the reader is advised to look after the excellent reviews that can be found in details on the internet. The original story was reported in a letter from 1754 but published with other stories later.

The three princes of Serendip *(Sri Lanka)*

The answer from the European scientist after the blossoming Age of Reason is given by Pasteur: "In the field of observation chance favors the prepared mind." The question is open for several interpretations, related to the general subject of uncertainty.

4.2. Late Evolution

Probability—each one can employ it; no one can take it away.
–Blaise Pascal, Thoughts: 913.

4.2.1. MATHEMATICS AS THE LAST COMPUTABLE FORM OF ANY SCIENCE

Here we have to make a small detour defending that rather awkward definition concerning science, mathematics, and computability. We speak about science, in the Anglo-American sense—i.e., science in the sense of reproducible, experimentally strong, provable phenomena, those having firm definitions for models of reproduction under defined conditions; and these model definitions are firm enough to be translated into regular formulae and mathematics. The last step is more obvious for the present view: based on the mathematical formulae, the model can be programmed and the outcome, the computational reproduction is computable.

The last statement clarifies the way of reasoning. First in physics, but now also in every practically manageable problem of biology-related medicine and agriculture, statistics and finance-related economy followed the overall dominating modern production processes of technology: computer-aided design, computer aided scheduling and manufacturing. All additional problems (remember the Aristotelian sumbebekos, i.e., the additional, secondary, and accidental) belong to some kind of uncertainty, not exactly definable and predictable incidents.

Experimental results, observations of phenomena and their contextual conditions are now interpreted by data, and these algorithmic-type interpretations supported by the contextual data are the firm constituents of modern, model based, computer processed scientific inference. The epistemic steps of model building and verification, explained in the first chapter's scheme, hypotheses, theories, more or less adequate models, are results of these algorithmic-type, data-structuring operations. The communication about any kind of scientific results belong to the first step of knowledge consolidation, the generation of hypothetical thoughts about other views, structures. Control of the international scientific community works on communication channels, communicating these algorithmic-type structuring methods and data structures. This is the procedure of any science now, humanistics more and more included. The statement about the procedural steps does not degrade the value of thoughts, communicated mainly in essays, put only the current, proved epistemic process in order.

The problem of truth verification received a new impulse due to the accelerated advancement of science and related revolutionary aspects, referred to before.

Where to start this story is an open question, too; should we start with the British Age of Reason or with Kant or later?

From our point of view, the 20th century is more interesting—the Vienna Circle and followers, Popper, Lakatos and the sociologist skeptic schools. Most of them tried to set firm definitions for acceptance, a typical reference should be the requirements of Popper about the necessity of a refutability program as a proof for impossibility of inverse statements. The idea of refutability was applied by the Greek mathematics and continuously later. How a new theory is able to incorporate novel contradictions, how they require some extensions of the theory and how revolutionary new theories should emerge, is always another evolutionary-type question decided later by science history. Let us remain with the pragmatic, constructive skeptic, with all its flexibility, renewable nature, and reliability by the freedom and multitude of science.

4.2.2. ARS CONIECTANDI, STATISTICS

Hacking's *The Emergence of Probability* (1975) tries to analyze the other reasons of the late emergence and the relevance of Pascal's and Jakob Bernoulli's contribution to the *ars coniectandi*, the art of dicing (and we add, the same Latin word is for reasoning based on a guess) and soon afterwards to the fast growing interest in problems, related to statistics in economy, social conditions, meteorology, and measurement in experiments on physical, chemical and biological phenomena.

The observation of returning frequencies and the estimation of future events are both connected and independent; the second developed more on the Bayesian conditional probability lines. The reference to the Bayesian is a consequence of remarks given just two paragraphs before. The Bayesian expresses the context of data, e.g., the part of the observed population, the temporal and local and other conditions of the data. These data about data are further subjected to critical review and algorithmic calculations, e.g., references to the temperature, pressure conditions, income, education and family relations of a certain population, and reliability of instrumentation. Every researcher or educated reader knows well this messy background of communicated data and therefore, all authentic scientific resources work hard on these analyses, their methodologies, on their influence, sensitivity ranges. The relatively free international web community and the developing rules due to freer competition create a never before existing check. With the multiple faces of freedom in research and freedom from earlier prejudices, canons are now manifested in the web-created society.

The detailed history of mathematical ideas about probability and the roles of great mathematicians are well detailed in the cited book by Hacking and many others, e.g., more recently by Halpern in 2003.

Models of uncertainty defined the progress of calculations. For a rather long time dicing and similar games have served as models. The way of observation developed statistics, and the contradiction between the fairly good approximations given for large numbers of experiments and the complete uncertainty of a single roll remained the epistemic curiosity.

Statistical models followed the hypotheses about the nature of the investigation. Typical are the distributions around a certain mean value, variations like the biological data of height, weight, life expectancy, etc.—both symmetric and not symmetric. Life expectancy in a certain advanced age is typically asymmetric.

Another model, used later for many purposes, is the reliability of selecting the best yielding varieties of barley for brewery. This was the *Student distribution*, measured on a limited number of samples. Here we meet another story: the applied mathematician *Student* (not so young, aged 32, at that time) who invented estimation statistics and was an employee chemist of the Guinness brewery, was pro-hibited to disclose his name, William Sealy Gosset, lest the method should be copied by other beer factories!

The problem is similar to the *Nala – Kali* story of mythology from India, that was cited just before. But now that it has received a firm scientific analysis and an idea—where to use and how to use? This re-mark puts light to the question, where does science start and where does sophisticated observation end. The other lesson refers to the socio-historical, technological environment of ideas, the story of Her-on's steam power invention returns innumerable times.

Heron of Alexandria was one of the great Greek scientists, math-ematicians and engineers, who invented the steam power and sev-eral other ingenious devices, wrote a book with the title *How to Con-struct Automata* and applied the feedback principle after his master Ktesibios (Lazos, 1993).

4.2.3. THE MODELS OF RANDOM MOTION

A series of models, rich in applications, started out of the collision problem of rigid and elastic objects. One of the first important mod-els is the *Brownian motion*. It was extended towards the more and more sophisticated variants with different border conditions, objects, e.g., elasticity, not only in physics but in the investigation of motion in human and other hysteric masses. For masses, events where motion is not primarily defined by collisions, the *Monte Carlo random-walk* model is applied best, as one of the main patterns of data mining or any other search in a field with completely unknown distribution. (See Appendix 2.6)

A further constraint of independence from previous events, or remembering only a fixed certain number of preliminaries, is the *Markovian model*, applied for instance in internet search engines. Among many other applications these methods work mostly in search on the internet, i.e., on huge amounts of information.

Experimental physics furnished the idea of *ergodicity*, which, in a simplified interpretation, the relation of similar experiments, equal chance for experimentation with one sample many times, or many samples. The theory of statistical mechanics was a model for thermo-dynamics and nuclear theory.

4.2.4. MODELS AS HYPOTHESES OR PREJUDICES

The models serve as hypotheses and prejudices, consciously or in a hidden way. The best example of an ideal model is the *Kolmogorov model* of probability.

Classic probability hypotheses work well in worlds, ensembles of events that can be modeled approximately by the constraints of the *Kolmogorov axioms*. On the other hand, in appropriate applications might be totally misleading, especially those related to relatively fast changing conditions and events, and not with constant frequencies. Typical examples are the stock exchange prices in hectic, crisis periods. Similar is the experience about mental and physical capabilities of significantly different ages and environments.

Kolmogorov clearly was, of course, aware of the limitations of the strict logico-mathematical axiomatic frames. The only difference, matured in the intermediate period, is the present weight of the external

Axiomatic closed world

realm, relevance in the computer age and its new approximation approaches, no less the theoretical relevance and well applied practical use of the Kolmogorov results.

As it looks like in the picture, we have a closed world, mutual independence, cumulative probabilities of occurrence and stationary time, according to the Kolmogorov axioms.

The circle looks really vicious: having a number of observations, we start to calculate evidence on the basis of a certain theoretical or experience-suggested model and get results that should be checked on the same hypothetical model or suggested by similar circumstances. The whole history of science can be recounted on this scheme. The only consolation that we can attribute as virtue, the practicality and power of science, is the continuous mass refinement of model approximations providing some more useful forecasts and approaches. The story of all, more or less, sophisticated technologies is the same, mass production and reproduction is the one of proofs, and the same is valid for progress in medicine, pedagogy, and economy.

Circularity (3.2.5) provokes another theoretical and practical problem of test procedures. Just a few lines before, speaking about the relevance of correct check, the emphasis was put on the reproduction and iteration under same conditions. This means just the possibility of a circular pitfall. In a control procedure—how to design the similarities and effects of dissimilarities—this is sometimes the serendipity case of experimenting talents who free the hypotheses from well proved conditions and push those into the garbage of prejudices.

Science can be considered as an infinite story of model approximations with the check of experimental improvement, receiving more justifications, more substantial forecasts.

4.2.5. An Uncertain Classification of Uncertainty

Returning to the different types of uncertainty, a rough and somehow arbitrary classification can be given:

  – Objective, physical uncertainty of the quantum world;
  – Uncertainty due to some existing but not yet discovered phenomena, e.g., causes and medicaments of some diseases;

– Uncertainty due to practically non-computable complexity, e.g., long-range, exact meteorological forecast;

– Uncertainty due to lack of knowledge, non-availability of data, and especially of historical events;

– Uncertainty due to unknown, unexpected interactions, especially human behavior;

– Uncertainty due to disinformation.

These different kinds of uncertainties can get a more definite classification after a clarification of the problem, i.e., after scattering the fog of uncertainty. The explanation of human behavior can be ordered into discovery of a neural disorder, due to the anticipation of a meteorological change, uncertainty about a not yet disclosed verdict and of the not yet discovered interactions in the brain. Seeing this enumeration, it is clear that in spite of any uncertainty typology for the conceptual generalization, different cases require different approximation models.

The model matching is sometimes more an art of serendipity than science of Nala and Kali, a capability of sensitivity for the opportunities and pitfalls of analogical thinking. Misleading analogies of mushroom appearance can be lethal, though not only the appearance but also many further qualities can be similar. The same is valid for algorithms and programs, being stable for a certain parameter and divergent for a small perturbation. The example for the necessary choice of new and strange looking models is the application of non-Euclidean geometries as models for the strange, uncertainty world of quantum physics.

All these are good reasons why scientists hated or abhorred uncertainty and why it is the great challenge of science now. The epistemic loop of observation remains the guide: creating hypotheses, based on observation analogies, affirmation of these hypotheses by new observations. The consolidation of that knowledge by theories is the progress route of current science, as was emphasized here several times.

Now, the difference with the past is the availability of immense observation data, the possibility to review their features by renewed and methodically revised observations. This loop is strengthened by the critical norms of unbiased science, its possible independence from ideological biases.

4.3. The Pragmatic View of Methodologies

A statement which is frequently and freely made, especially before the matter was as well analyzed as it is now, is that there is some contrast between things that are subject to strict mathematical treatment, and things which are left to chance.

...

And again it takes a mathematical treatment to realize that if an event is not determined by strict laws, but left to chance, as long as you have clearly stated what you mean by this (and it can be clearly stated) it is just as amenable to quantitative treatment as if it were rigorously defined.

...

The theory of probability furnishes an example for this.

John von Neumann, "The Role of Mathematics in the Sciences and in Society"

4.3.1. METHODOLOGICAL CLASSIFICATION

From our point of view we emphasize two relevant features of the process: the critical and pragmatic attitude of the methodologies and the computer science support of data management, especially data mining.

Methodologies are only enumerated here. They are well discussed in excellent textbooks and university courses. The enumeration serves the overview of practical but not general devices as a set of tools for manufacturing different shaped surfaces (Vámos, 1991).

– Statistics, with its temporal, conditional dependence constraints and evaluation methods (Savage, 1954; UCLA, probability and statistics e-book);

– Classic probability, with its definitional constraints and developments for calculating the effects of disturbing these constraints (Bertsekas, Tsitsiklis, 2008);

– Bayesian methods for conditional probabilities, estimations with combination of statistical, probabilistic data. The epistemic peculiarity from classic probability was treated in this chapter (Pearl, 1998, 2000);

– Possibility methods (e.g., Dempster-Shafer, certainty factor, etc.) with attention to the combinations of statistics, probability concepts, and anomalies related to cumulating marginal estimations (Shafer, 1976, Shafer-Logan, 1987);

– Fuzzy methods for estimating memberships within hypothetical or real groups of instances, a major method for using human estimations and neglecting uncertain relations of distributions. In its non-probabilistic view the method has a different course in acceptance and applications (Zadeh, 1965);

– Various methods for estimating the dynamics of stochastic processes. These are basic subjects of all control and system-science studies, the majority of publications and textbooks appear under the identification issue.

All these methods have some natural roots in set theory–dealing with hypothetical sets of data, instances, and qualifications. These methods also have roots in algebra and logic, due to the tasks of combination uncertainty data. All these methods, sooner or later, receive increasing attention to the problem of evidence, based on measurement data and on human estimation. Even the theoretically strongest classic probability theory had a rather early branch, called subjective probability.

In our previous work (Vámos, 1991) and elsewhere in literature, the denominations, such as probability, vagueness, possibility, evidence, estimation are used in different contexts. The same denomination appears in strictly defined separate meanings. This variety of definitions and naming reflects the intrinsic nature of uncertainty. For better orientation references to the origin and reliability of data, the discussion of the calculation method and measures of data confidence are major requirements.

4.3.2 WHERE ARE WE NOW?

The greatest difference to the earlier situation of science was underlined:

– The availability of reliable, wide-range instrumentation previously not in existence, increasing the possibilities of human observation by about thirty magnitudes from fento- to tera-measures and even further;

– The possession of a never before imaginable amount of observational data and computational power, as well as mathematical methods for management;

– Retrieval of information and data by means of machine learning;

– A continuously developing epistemic discipline for critical revisions of hypotheses and theories, consciousness of liberty and independence in the permanent struggle against interests alien to science;

– The global society of modern science, cooperating via powerful channels of communication and the emerging rules, guidelines, and ethics of this cooperation burdened by all traditional and new disorders of human nature.

4.3.3. Data Mining

Data mining is a collective designation of all modern methods for discovery of connections and structures among seemingly unstructured data. The first answer was the application of classic methods in statistics: significance, factors, etc. Soon it turned out that, if the multitude of data and points for hypothetical order is very huge, then these methods are mostly insufficient, the relations more hidden than–according to the popular saying–a needle in a haystack. The escape route returned to the model hypotheses but in a conscious way of checking the hypotheses.

The challenge mobilized a wide variety of mathematical disciplines. The most frequently applied methods are the *hidden Markovian procedures*, search for returning phrases, expressions, contexts. From this short reference it is visible that sophisticated connection searches should apply several tricks, hypothetical schemes, and a possibly comprehensive expertise within the special subject concerned.

Data mining is in most cases equivalent with a search for hidden patterns and structures behind the patterns. Mathematics is, in some sense, the theory of structures, a search for structures, and a building of structures. All disciplines of mathematics can be interpreted in

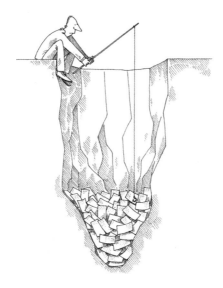

Data mining

that way and this generalization helps the continuous interplay within the realm of mathematics, especially between geometry, its further abstractions, like topology and all others—algebra, algebraic foundations of logic, analysis, etc.

The search for structures in data is a search within the certain branch of science and practice, related to technology or any phenomena of nature, the human being included. If we accept this interpretation, the search can be understood as application of knowledge about abstracted structures applied to the investigated discipline and in between the method and the special discipline, the hypothetical model. These selected models are the guesses of the solution hypotheses and further some guiding hints to the possibly independent methods of hypothesis control. By possibly independent, we refer to the model itself and the computational procedure, too.

The search applies the old usual methods, too; i.e., analysis, matching data to some basic functions of temporal behavior, clustering, classification, frequency analysis and related methods based on the classical methods and on different waveforms, like wavelets and fractals. These methods are in some sense closest to the model view, to the evolutionary exponential and to the logarithmic decay, to powers of energy relations and further, well known actions and interactions of complicated motion or frequencies of all kinds of oscillations and returning phenomena.

Functional analysis as a mathematical discipline appears to provide tools for finding in some sense a model for the best looking class of functions and by that a reverse reasoning to the nature of the data scheme, the model. The application of functional equations in approximation search is a recent attempt in mining economy and psychology data (Aczél, 2000).

Fitting a polynomial function on coordinated data is a fundamental meaning of algebraic operations, as we have seen earlier in Chapter 2.

4.3.4. Spaces of Events and Search

The first model and even linguistic metaphor is geometry. The fantasy-rich development of Riemann surfaces, non-Euclidean geometry, topology (Gromov, 1999), and the new world of related metrics is the most promising present and future field of model building and search procedures on these strange, multidimensional spaces. These spaces are strange for a traditional view of a human culture, first attached only to the two-dimensional surface of a flat looking earth and slowly accustomed to a similar view in the third dimension.

Modern science has shown that nature is not as unimaginative as we were. The strange multidimensional, topological space is really the dynamic representation of nature, not only of the far cosmological one but representing all kinds of internal and external phenomena, those not understood until now.

Not understood is a highly relative attribute. The models and so the spaces of present science are rather strictly bound to our early visual impressions; and though they are beautiful and admirable further abstractions, they are "only" expressions of relations in our language. Language means also abstractions of natural language towards any means of representation.

The vicious circle has pragmatic solutions. The models are understood in that working sense; they are accepted as long as they are in conformance with the data and observations. Data mining is the search for a good model, good in adjustment to the data, in coherence with other related knowledge, and with the possibility of computational application. Model means in this respect the relative understanding of a position within the general world of current knowledge. It is nothing more in the view of final totality and nothing less than an admirable instrument of everyday life, of orientation in the complexity of the practical world.

4.3.5. Restitution of Approximations, the Sorcerer's Hulls

The next remark concerns the approximation itself. The origins of mathematics, for a long time, have been the art of approximations—approximations in the sense of calculating everyday phenomena. Especially after the revolutionary achievements of science in the 19th century, approximation for mathematics was a kind of dirty, fuzzy practice, not the world of elegant mathematical theory. This view changed once more in the previous decades.

The change is due to the dramatic development of computer power and in connection with this, a new horizon of the earlier limits of practical and theoretical computability, considered theoretical

Schrödinger's cat, without the hull of quantum- state mystic!

only. As stated before, one kind of uncertainty is the limit of computability, because of the exponential or even faster growth of complexity. *This type of uncertainty emerged to be a major obstacle, possibly, the major obstacle.* All others, related to the unknown, undiscovered, and misunderstood phenomena are or can be the subjects of further investigations and new experimental and theoretical ideas–they are open challenges for research. Even the most quoted example of objective uncertainty, the Schrödinger state-measurement puzzle, is or can be an emerging problem from the realm of mystery to experimentation and further application in computing.

High complexity, problems beyond the current physical computability limits are of a different nature. The mathematical background, the nature of problems where the models are unavoidably beyond the limits of polynomial time solutions, and the classes of these hard algorithmic problems are now the subject of excellent university textbooks, not to be detailed here (Hromkovic, 2002).

The efforts for model transformations are, until now, partly limited to the purposes of several important real cases, how to interpret some non-polynomial models as polynomials, matched especially to the requirements of algorithmic computational operations. The broad analogy class of the celebrated *traveling salesman problem* belongs to those. (See: 4.3.8) A great many of environmental and mental subjects lie certainly beyond the same, in the practical infinities of computational steps. The difference between practical and theoretical computability is emphasized, the first refers to the fast growing capabilities of current technology, the second to the conceptual realms discussed in the chapter about algebra and are due, first of all, to the theorems of Gödel and Turing. New possibilities of technologies, methods of computation, and practical limits of our physical world lie in between.

If we accept the theses about the modeling role of mathematics for any problem treatable scientifically, and in conclusion about the manageability of all those by computation, then we find the new limit of knowledge in the computability problem. In short: *if not computable, then it is not manageable by the firm reproducible methods of rational science.*

This statement should be taken also with salt and pepper. A well reproducible experimental result, if it may not be inserted into a general scheme of theoretical context, can be a highly relevant problem, suggesting further research and theoretical revisions.

Sentences like this are not utterly satisfactory for any kind of rational, goal-oriented human intellect. That is the main reason why approximation reached a new status in rigorous science. In this way, as a natural feedback, great new theories, mathematical instruments of approximation calculi, and the confidence algorithms of those emerged. The best example is the development of topology-related methods, creation of possibly convex hulls around the feasible solutions, reduction, transformation of these hulls into manageable dimensions and patterns. Manageable means realistic conditions of computation and of pattern matching. The last refers to analogy thinking, finding similarities, measures of similarity and dissimilarity. All these new mathematical methods are, on the one hand, delicacies by their highly sophisticated nature, perceivable only to the most erudite mathematical brains. On the other hand, the elaborated programming instruments based on these novelties come to work in a fast progress as practical tools for routine engineering design. All problems of non-linear and stochastic nature, which is the practical case for most engineering tasks, are somehow covered by these sorcerer's hulls.

The idea of demonstrating mathematical proofs by computational experimentation was accepted similarly. This has a very relevant practical meaning as well, not only for the development of mathematics, but in the mirror of the above applications: a new instrument for validity, confidence estimations, a key problem for engineering design. As a milestone of this development, since 1992, there is a separate and by now highly regarded scientific journal titled *Experimental Mathematics*.

Not completely independent is the renaissance of number theory as a new, stimulating subject in modern cryptography and in general search procedures for structures in huge data masses. Apparent connection points are the ancient problems of prime numbers, the somehow mystic elementary building blocks of all numbers, and by this merit of hidden keys and hidden structures. The secrecy of the keys is a routine requirement of the whole society, the discovery of hidden structures is an objective of most research problems, e.g., pharmaceutical chemistry and genetics.

4.3.6. Compromise: Inclusion of Human Estimates and Conclusions about the Ubiquity of Research

Another novelty under the hull of uncertain phenomena is also an unorthodox development: calculations pertaining to human-influenced processes. The guess of subjectivities is unavoidable in economy, in negotiations of other types, and in planning strategies in complex actions. Two hypotheses and some other results won Nobel Prizes in analyzing the human decision process. The first group is characterized by the modern continuation of the classical Adam Smith school of rational choice, later enriched by Weber, Parsons, Buchanan and Tullock, and many further authors. The other major trend is marked by the psychology-based groups, characterized by the works of Kahnemann, Slovic, Tversky, and their followers. All these are flavored by the *Condorcet-Arrow* line of proof for the impossibility of optimal choice among several different, well-founded interests and of an unobjectionable voting system.

These developments were applied in the frames of the game theories initialized by Borel and von Neumann and in the historical beginnings of optimization, dating back to the 18th century. The theories of reasonable compromises and balances—started by Pareto and in our age, von Neumann, Nash, Harsányi, Black and Scholes, Aumann and Schelling, Myerson, Hurwitz and Maskin—mention the Nobel class of economy only (Myerson, 1991). The Founding Fathers, Borel and von Neumann, were active before the Nobel Prize was extended for economy, and mathematics have only recently been given prizes at this level. The future developments should underline more the relevance of the enumerated individuals' achievements.

The main problem was, and is still, the balance among different attitudes, objectives, and environments. A combination of rational strategies and motivations of individuals and various masses is needed. Present circumstances and the several hundred-million-year-old evolutionary heritage of the human animal get into conflict. This immense task of present human existence and coexistence demonstrates the ubiquity of uncertainty, and the relevance of its research, the intrinsic complexity, due above all to the natural coherence of all related scientific disciplines. The contradictions look to be unsolvable, all rational or less rational ideals of a society safe of

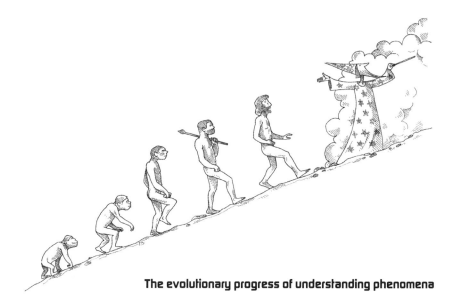

The evolutionary progress of understanding phenomena

contradictions failed due to the inexpugnable motivations of mankind. These are, as a matter of fact, the same as listed by the psychological remarks of Aristotle, and this is the very reason why we understand and enjoy the Greek or the Shakespearean tragedies, timeless after so many centuries.

Modern game theory and psychology try to manage the balance and unbalance phenomena of decisions. The resulting models should approach these disequilibria, their dynamics and possibly quasioptimal control. The story of the recent economic world crisis demonstrates the poverty of the earlier celebrated models and the necessity of less biased, more complex research.

4.3.7. LIMITS OF UNCERTAINTY

The border of randomness and determinism is by definition uncertain. Even the fundamental question of randomness in a sequence of integers was an open question. Kolmogorov gave the witty definition for that, cited in 3.2.4: "If there is no algorithm shorter than the sequence, the sequence is random." The proof of this nonexistence of a shorter algorithm is a further problem. The methods determining the conditions of experiments were discussed earlier, statistics and other data acquisition methods developed their specific estimates for estimating accuracy and certainty. Think of the population composition and multitude of opinion polls required to estimate a decision.

Choosing a model is not a task in pure mathematics, but it evolves in cooperation with experts of the application discipline. It is a really deep epistemic problem. The result is mostly double: an applicable model for the discipline concerned and a new mathematical result extending the methods and ways of thinking in mathematics.

Some examples show the diversity of these relative novelties. Relative novelty, as discussed at many issues here, is also a vague definition, here applied, in the past one or two decades, to the new problems and possibilities evoked by computer science.

4.3.8. SOME EXAMPLES OF ALGORITHMIC SUCCESS

As mentioned the *traveling salesman problem* is a general metaphor of linear programming, solving most of the optimization tasks among well-defined alternatives and subordinated to constraints. The absolute solution is a prototype of efficiently non-computable complexity. The first successful approximation algorithm of Dantzig, published after WWII, was the mapping of the problem into a vertex of a polyhedron, and walking along its edges using successive approximation values.

Interior-point methods started with Khachiyan in 1979. His results were mostly of theoretical value, using an ellipsoid boundary instead of the polyhedron. The walking took place, after finding a feasible interior point, within the problem volume. In 1984, Karmarkar proposed a new interior point method with a predictor-corrector, i.e., extrapolation and step control mechanism.

The generality of the linear programming idea extends the application field from conventional optimization to any model of approximation of best decisions, best from very different points of view and having previously set or random realization constraints.

– *Kernels and Factorization (referred to in: 2.4.4., 2.4.5., 3.1.5.)*

The other flourishing field of approximation algorithms is factorization, decomposition of complex effects to basic components which

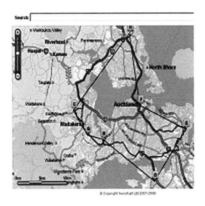

The traveling salesman problem

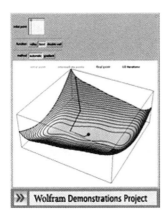

Wolfram Demonstrations Project

Interior-point methods

can be handled more separately. This means decomposition to practically mutually independent and simple partitions. We need this possibility from cryptography to models of complex industrial and economy processes, everywhere having many data and measurements forming a kind of lattice within the multidimensional space of numbers, phenomena, and states.

After many previous results the LLL–Lenstra, Lenstra, Lovász–algorithm could yield a relatively fast and predictably correct solution, transforming the vector space of the given data into projections closely orthogonal and relatively short, i.e., into a more easily treatable form of mutually independent components.

– Physics, Quantum, and Evolutionary Computing (See Appendix 3.3)

The model family of physics is currently a challenging field of algorithmic development. Physics was always a stimulating origin of mathematical ideas. Now, quantum phenomena open a new chapter called already quantum computation, although the theoretical and practical possibilities of realizations are currently uncertain.

– Other Computational Models: Tessellation, Fluid Dynamics (more in Chapter 2)

New results in tessellation, tiles, and fractals, i.e., in geometric morphology and in some features of *Brownian motion*, added to previous computational efforts for representing turbulent, chaotic movement of human and non-human masses strengthen the cardinal hypothesis about order and disorder in nature: the evolutionary dynamics of non-living and living material develops on the border of regularity and irregular uncertainty (Penrose, 1974, 2004).

Developmental dynamics creates the regularities and "laws" of nature—seemingly rule-organized phenomena. The mathematical model investigations and search algorithms for representation of these dynamics work consciously and non-consciously along that borderline. It is expressed also in the asymptotic behavior of the efficient approximation algorithms, in the prevalence of some critical data and numbers. Critical data are present in fundamental constants of physics and critical numbers in their theory, like the prime numbers, and in geometry. Ramsey proved a certain general order in any, possibly disordered, structure.

The intrinsic relations of randomness and order in the universe and in the developmental history of life returned regularly from the early mythologies to recent theories. Let us refer to the Genesis story of our culture and to the works of The Santa Fe Institute, especially by (Kaufman, 1993).

The development of those self-orientation processes usually follows the interactions of individual random phenomena and creates an existential possibility of interaction results, mostly to some extreme-valued states. The concept of entropy and the abundance of entropy-modeled processes is a good example. Entropy stems from the random Brownian thermodynamic behavior and is a fundamental model not only in thermodynamics but also information theory, as well as several biological and social models. The *simulated annealing* model idea used for optimization-approximation algorithms is also related to the thermal model (Whitfield, 2005).

Returning to *quantum computation*, from our point of view, the generation of admirably sophisticated new algorithms is relevant. They carry the lesson of an ever self-renewing and results-breeding mathematical instrumentation. We receive a promise for solving or approximating hidden phenomena, sufficiently and reliably, enriching knowledge and especially knowledge by computing. The second lesson is the sophistication ladder to complexity that looks to be step-by-step longer, requiring more devoted effort from mathematicians. The proofs of these new algorithms are growing in length and depth, and are hard to catch. That lesson advocates for the relevance and respect to be given to these efforts.

The engineering aspect of quantum computation is very exciting—the challenge of building a quantum computer as a real computing device.

The next lesson is our returning epistemic pragmatism. The approximation algorithms are easily converted to ready-made programs available in advanced program libraries. The difficult transparency of their mathematical background can cover the caveats of application limitations for the selection of appropriate instruments. Linear programming, for instance, is an everyday practical task for any optimization but the questions of which algorithms are adequate and where, and which ones are not, and how to mix them in a complicated program, are questions that belong to the art of mathematical and practical programming. The way we engage in more and more complex tasks in any science and science-based practice remains an art.

.

CHAPTER 5

Excursion to the Fields of Ontology, Being and Beliefs

Freuet euch des wahren Scheins,
Euch des ernsten Spieles!
Kein Lebend'ges ist ein Eins,
Immer ist's ein Vieles.

The true illusion celebrate,
Be joyful in the serious game!
No living thing lives separate:
One and Many are the same.

Goethe, *Epirrhema*, second strophe

5.1. Ontology, Homunculus, Constructive Skepticism

The problems around uncertainty reach the border of epistemology and *ontology*. Ontology is understood here in the original philosophical sense–philosophy of Being.

The ontology question arose much before the times of modern robots and related computer intelligence: is man able to create an artificial homunculus, a *Golem* which is, in affective and cognitive respects, similar or even mightier than a natural human? Mysticism of the Middle Ages was a fertile soil for these ideas. The *Homunculus* in the Christian world and the *Golem* in the Judaic world both developed later to widely used symbolic figures in literature.

By the advent of computer intelligence, the idea of a technologically feasible artificial intelligence was an obvious continuation of these mystical imaginations. Even the name *robot*, originated in 1920 by the Čapek brothers in Karel's futuristic-satiric novel, was born at the temporal border of the classical industrial period and the proliferation of automatic control technology. Later, until now and surely after, science fiction and philosophy treat the question as a favorite popular agenda, now based on really impressive results of machine intelligence. The related literature, movies and other media can fill a comprehensive library.

Those who foresee a feasible computer-driven android refer to the present achievements of programs, having comparable, or even better results in certain intelligent tasks with respect to the best of human professionals. Chess is only one of these examples, but solving complex navigation, recognition, manipulation tasks is really impressive; several sensory inputs perform more reliably and with higher accuracy than human organs do.

The vision of bridging the orders-of-magnitude gap between the complexity estimates of the brain and of machine capacities is supported by the well-advertised "laws" of technological progress, like the Moore Law of chip performance. They have proved to be valid for a remarkable period, and in these forecasts are prolonged, extrapolated for a not too far possibility.

I do not discuss here the numeric estimate of these complexities, due to the complexity of the brain, which is not yet appraised. The number of neurons does not yet have a rather reliable estimate, neither their synaptic and non-synaptic connections, nor the ways and modes of electrical and chemical communication; it can reach a level of magnitude in the high teens. The weight of operational speed is also a fuzzy and a greatly task-dependent issue. On the other hand, the capabilities and realization possibilities of unconventional or quantum computation is also an uncertain future.

Both the brain and the machine can achieve in the practical sense infinite numbers of state, much beyond the present and foreseeable computational limits. The cardinality of the machine states can be estimated rigorously, less for this order of finiteness for the brain. This is the reason why the brain-machine problem cannot be decided from this mechanical direction. Ontologically it belongs to the pragmatic realm of agnosticism.

The other approach touches an even deeper problem of our being. That is the question, quoted after many antecedents, by Gauguin: "Where are we coming from? What are we? Where are we going?"

The fundamental difference between the two developments is a teleological construction story of the machine and the non-teleological, evolutionary development of the brain. The brain contains in its superposing, interacting complexity most of the intermediate archeological pragmatisms of our animal, proto-human and present history. Good or bad, as all our affective mechanisms are, these are expressed best in arts, and *that* is human! It has no meaning to and for any other living creatures, neither for robots. We can like it or hate it, as all these reveal themselves always and every day, working in our Self and all kinds of communities.

This ontological picture is a rather firm and lasting reality. Judgment about and above it lies beyond our epistemology, it is an everlasting question of philosophy. Several thinkers refer to the necessity of a superhuman judgment and possible salvation; others accept the pragmatic reality and mix it with socio-political salvation ideologies. They always proved to be as metaphysical as the theological responses.

This is not a comprehensive history of philosophy and therefore no author is quoted. On the other hand, we must be aware of the fact that in engineering, i.e., in a man-machine symbiotic world, we must feel the individual and common responsibility of the manifestations of Being—good and bad, ancient and new.

As Norman, an "emotional designer," stated in the January 2004 issue of the Scientific American, the motifs of the question:

Why machines should fear?

5.2. Ethics: Our Pragma— Useful and Necessary

This is the *pragma* of our epistemic and ontological aspects, formulated mostly in views about ethics. Ethics is also understood in its complete philosophical-pragmatic context—morals, laws, other regulations, habits and fashions, communication games in their Wittgensteinian sense. If we refer only to the relations between individual citizens and their local and global communication and regulation systems, most incorporated into the frames of information networks, we can estimate the conceptual weight of conscious deliberation.

My attitude, and not my answer, is a kind of *constructive skepticism*, not far from that of Rorty's. It stems from the epistemic methodology of Aristotle, the relativistic criticism of the ancient Skeptics and the moral thinking of Spinoza and Mill. These names mark milestones "only" in an infinite line of possibly bias-free questioning of the self and of the environment. The view serves also as a reminder to the attitude of modesty, personal and professional responsibility. Dealing with computer epistemology belongs to these modest and responsible engineering duties.

The attitude is a kind of *constructive skepticism*, as the intension of the book indicates. The name returns several times in the history of philosophy, in economy, medical praxis, psychology and pedagogy, maybe elsewhere. It is related mostly to the thoughts of the Age of Reason, first of all to Gassendi and later to the cited British rationalists. The same notion was used for familiar thoughts on theology, starting with the revision of the *Abelardian* idea of a rational causation for the concept of God, and continued by reform theologies within the Catholic Church and the Reformation. One of the original authors was Francisco Sanchez, an Iberian philosopher of Jewish origin at the turn of the 16th and 17th century, a refugee from the Inquisition, who was possibly the first to use the term constructive skepticism.

The ways of thinking for more or less rationalist philosophers and practitioners of many disciplines are logical continuations of the compromise attitude. This is characterized by a skeptic knowledge about our current and further possible limitations but with certain esteem of the human progress until our days. *Constructive skepticism*, a moderate optimist approach, tries to construct a possible and feasible progress, never complete and perfect, but mostly and probably an improvement.

Computer Epistemology is an especially relevant branch of this long trend and attitude, due to the ubiquity of information technology.

The striking controversy of the anti-Aristotelian standpoints of the constructive skepticisms and our admiration of Aristotle as one of the founders of our ways of thinking will be the subject of the next paragraphs. The ethical lesson is the other point.

5.3. Analytic Versus Metaphysical, Logic Versus Pattern

The rather philosophical and science-fiction-related homunculus problem has a very practical aspect. Using computer-controlled and -assisted systems, the Wittgensteinian word should mean that what cannot be defined and logically-algorithmically deduced should be avoided. The results of any kind of non-logical computation are uncertain.

The essential message of the after-Gödelian models, as quoted here several times, is as well the impossibility of this exclusive fixation. The main practical treatment is the acknowledgment and steady checking of the logically closed world limits, as it is used in non-monotonic logic methods. This is what we do in the application of any computer program.

The challenge of transgressing these limits, practiced also by Wittgenstein, is a compromise-excursion to the field covered traditionally by metaphysics. In science this was mostly treated by psychology. This discipline, which originally used to be mere philosophy- and humanistics-related, is now more and more approaching the professional features of science. It is supported by neurobiology, evolutionary biology, and statistical mathematics. In computer science that transition means an analogical methodology, *computational linguistics* of semantic and semiotic analysis, and pattern-related knowledge.

The key concept is *pattern* and pattern analogy. All affective, psychological phenomena and abilities are, according to our present views, pattern-like. Interests, emotions, ingenuity of finding new connections, hypotheses about interactions are all represented as patterns in our imaginary mental structures. Patterns are represented by bunches of individual data, connecting graphs among them and by multidimensional data-spaces covering the somehow coherent-looking data. The real neurobiological representation is still unclear, though certain localities and dynamics are identified which work in typical tasks in the brain. The philosophical speculations about the singular, biochemical operation or dual, biochemical and spiritual mind are not decided, maybe this will be never finally closed. In our computation-oriented view the reason of this undecidability is not really spiritual but due basically to computational complexity.

Patterns of structures are emerging models for several social and biological phenomena. These are mostly modeled by graphs, their random behavior and qualities can reflect from some developmental points of view the optimal developments of connections. Some similarities can be found in the structures of vascular systems, neural connections and behavior or, more exactly, the diameter of the network of human masses. The maximal number of human relational contacts was the idea of the ingenious Hungarian author Karinthy in 1929. (Barabási, 2002; Érdi, 2008.)

For further details and illustrations go back to the second chapter.

The choice of computing devices, digital or analogical, is a more interesting problem in that case. Several ideas and experiments emerged during the past half a century for combination; application of more neural-like nets does not close the development in any final way, though until now, due to flexibility, production technologies and continuously increasing capabilities in hardware and software ensured a high priority to digital computation.

The mathematical-computational discipline of pattern recognition, based on geometrical analogies, data mining, advanced statistical and algorithmic methods, linguistic analysis focusing on grammatical and semantic coherence, are all currently fast emerging research and application areas. The growing motivation for these is due to the rapid development of computational methods in all kinds of ever-growing technological complexities, communication, information processing, medical practice, and social networks. The dimensions can be visualized in the existence and growth of the Google-like mega-organizations, their gigantic computational, information retrieval, and financial power.

The background of this emergence is the conscious and only partly unconscious acknowledgement of the non-detachable human aspect of man, serving these systems. These systems are less and less detachable, compared to earlier man and tool relations.

Essentially, this is a revolutionary change in the many-millennia-lasting relation of man and tool.

5.4. Future Human Roles and Attitudes, and Constructive Skepticism

The revolution sharpens the open problem of the new human roles, and this is, in conclusion, the main social problem of a still developing mankind (Vámos, 1981, 1983). The revolution illuminates the epistemic questions of this book: the growing necessity of a wide and concrete view of possibilities and limitations of each computational instrument. The unavoidable introduction of human-role-related uncertain elements suggests the current and probably lasting answer to the earlier, only philosophical dichotomy. It is not a question of ideologies, beliefs, but the *pragma* itself. Therefore, it is monistic in computer programming in its scientific methods and actions, and with the continuous pragmatic skepticism, incorporated into research and application areas.

Skepticism, the critical view of knowledge and knowledge-based reasoning, in its long history from Pyrrhon via his Greek followers and interpreters, the Roman Seneca, the British Hume and modern skeptics, all refer to the same arguments. These arguments are anchored in the human nature, motivations, not too much changed during the two and a half millennia of that long historical period.

Many of the skeptic thinkers conclude in a pessimistic world view, rejecting all, or most of, beliefs in any higher teleological principle and embodied force. This way leads to a kind of nihilism and, first of all, in Nietzsche to a new kind of mysticism around the human power.

The other branch, especially the British school of philosophy, demonstrate the social influence of reasoning. In contrast to the prevailing German tradition, they all are, more or less, fathers and children of Enlightenment, and put a positive emphasis on the conclusions about the possibility of an emergent freethinking, rationalistic mankind.

All these philosophies motivated by the Age of Reason are deeply ethical, deducing ethics from the comprehension of a mutually optimal human attitude and, therefore, they are moderate optimists.

Not quoting this long sequence of great thinkers and mostly great ethical human characters, I refer to Hume only, who could be the best example of this positive answer to the external uncertainty. That is the reason why Rorty was mentioned as characteristic of the contemporary philosophy, and we started with an evolutionary analysis of our erudite thinking.

Characterizing the two schools of philosophy by their national belonging is, of course, a brute generalization (think, e.g., of Kant) but it is, on the other hand, a reference to rather clear socio-historical environments.

The consequent answer of British freethinking was the dominance of analytical philosophy, the acceptance only of well-proven experimental facts, and reasoning based on the natural lines of logic. This perspective was an obvious continuation of Aristotle's syllogistic universalism. Analytical philosophy came into natural collision with the other answer to uncertainty, with the metaphysical escape from reality and progress. History and especially science of the present times put these controversies into their historical frames and pay tribute to the ambiguities. It is also an absolution for our myopia.

Computer epistemology is well suited for moderately optimistic, internally driven ethical skepticism. The quality of optimistic is based on the fantastic progress of modern science and, its direct and indirect fruits, such as, the doubling of enjoyable lifespan within about a hundred or more years. Many great problems disappeared for a great part of the world, such as famine and cold, need for human beings working as draught animals, and the conscious fight for preserving Nature. All are proved in the part of the world where our discipline could realize its blessings. The counter lesson is where modern technology, due to historical reasons, could not yet prevail!

Constructive skepticism is moderately optimistic, seeing the other face of reality, not only in the less advanced countries. Most maladies, among them some motivations which were driving forces of our celebrated progress, are bound to the fundamental evils of human nature.

Constructive skepticism is an attitude and activity, consideration of constraints and knowledge-based extension of constrained limits. In that view, it is an ethical stance, too.

CHAPTER 6

Conclusions

1. Computation and information technology started a radical change in human relations to all kinds of work and communication by the introduction of their technological instruments.

2. This injection introduces the necessity of translating all computer-mediated tasks into the language of computers. The language of computers, programming, is a direct translation of mathematics. This means: most human activities are to be formalized by the instruments of mathematics.

3. Mathematics, used in this vital formulation as a modeling procedure, is based on the principles of algebra, in a hierarchical abstraction similar to evolution, starting with a few basic conceptual components and rules. Logic and handling uncertainty follow these principal avenues.

4. The multistage translation process carries the continuous dangers of distortions and omitting details, relevant in unforeseen situations. The necessity of careful checks in all intermediate steps, in application adequacy of methods, mathematical modeling, and programming instruments, is growing.

5. Depending on the role and responsibility of the procedures, this critical, feedback-oriented view emerges as a vital requirement. Feedback is directed to the phenomena of the observable reality, without bias of earlier prejudices. These traditional principles of science emerge as pragmatic survival conditions and relate, practically, to the whole human race of modern civilization. This is the essence of a computer-oriented epistemology and the ethics of a constructive skeptic world view.

The great discovery

Appendices

1.1. Integrated Control of Vehicles and Traffic

The motivations create a partly conflicting manifold of objectives. Fuel prices and therefore design principles of the engine, grip of the wheels, aerodynamic body can be typical. Safety objectives add several further requirements for body structure, acceleration, and control and brake performance. Social relations of the market define pricing, comfort, representation of status, and age. Professional, family and other lifestyle aims should be added to that. Protecting the environment is now a major point of view. Production technology, expected volumes, and interchangeable parts for different car classes, economy, and production control of mass issue should be harmonized with fast delivery of partly individual customer compliance.

All these requirements are concentrated within the overall and local control systems of up-to-date vehicles. The example of these systems illustrates the complex nonlinear, stochastic control of steering, fuel (acceleration, deceleration, energy-storage regime) and brake, with suspension control of the car body. These continuous, mostly automatic control systems should realize a possibly ideal cooperation with the human driver, considering the different drivers' various driving characteristics. The direct driving system is more and more combined with the smart knowledge-based systems of the vehicle and of the road system. This means inter alia knowledge about road signals, road information systems, aerodynamic and vehicle stability situations, related sensory hardware and algorithms, visual pattern-recognition and sensory road-quality identification with related control knowledge. The design optimizes all interactive and conflicting objectives of safety, economy, and speed. The knowledge base should be able to store and retrieve histories of experienced traffic situations.

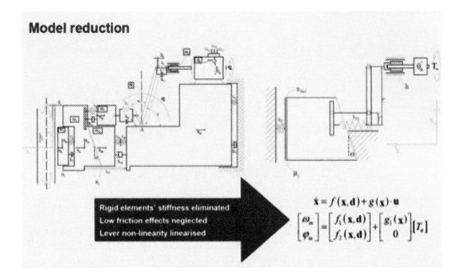

The simplified model of suspension

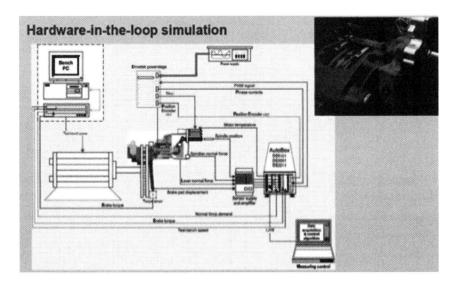

The driving mechanisms

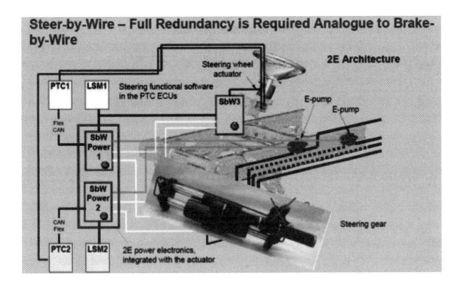

The brake-by-wire system

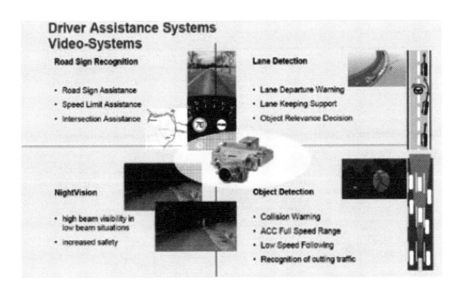

The intelligent vision-driver assistance

This highly complex system requires a well-balanced design of the individual controls and of their harmonic, partly cooperative, partly hierarchically organized operation and measures for any possible deficiencies of the system. Practically all problems of human-machine individual and social control organizations, all their technical and social-philosophical aspects are concentrated within this task, used for an example of our specific subject. A few schemes illustrate some connections, the first about *the simplified model of suspension*, the second about *the driving mechanisms*, the third about *the brake-by-wire system,* the fourth about *the intelligent vision-driver assistance.*

1.2. Scheduling

Scheduling of complex production chains is an NP-hard task, and according to our knowledge, non-computable in polynomial time if we would consider all possible variations of the schedule. The figure is a nice sketch of all participants of the process.

The chain can start with raw-material orders, and following their transport, the technological production (if all preliminary steps of technology such as design, machining etc. are given), scheduling of production machines and personnel, testing and warehousing,

The brake-by-wire system

packaging, and delivery to sales organizations. All these should be considered with related uncertainties and risks. The schedule should have short-range, long-range, and emergency perspectives. The entire chain is bound by telecommunication and transport links.

The task is, consequently a game problem among diverse, unreliable, differently oriented agents, challenging the most advanced methods of game situation and bargaining models.

A practical instance of the problem, which we solved at our Institute, involves the following fixed parameters:

The dimensions of a manufacturing part in a working system can be estimated by its currently available 145 machines, 764 job orders, within those 5,116 different jobs, all for the next week's operative schedule.

The program has to handle a lot of asymmetric information in the game, the manufacturer is well aware of their own resources, expenses, warehouses, and has very unreliable information about the momentary market, the speculations of the wholesale partners, and no information about uncertainties of possible emergency cases. Finding appropriate game and bargaining models, the distribution of risk and taking into consideration similar cases and earlier experiences are all included into the task.

The problem is, in its overall extension, practically non-computable due to its complexity, and due to the unsolvable problem of overall optimization among different values and interests. The high level mathematical modeling and experimentation challenge is finding approximations, aggregations of items, jobs, negligible items, and agreed peggings for acceptable *modus vivendi*.

A short description illustrates a part of an overall mathematical model:

The scheduling problem

The *input data* of our scheduling problem can be summarized as follows:

there is a set of *job families* $\{J_1,...J_n\}$, where J_i requests the production of a specific end-product or intermediate-product in a given quantity $\bar{q}_i$. Each J_i has a *release date* r_i and a *due date* d_i. Each J_i is divided a priori into a finite number of *jobs*, where job $j \in J_i$ represents the production of q_j items from J_i.

Note that $\sum_{j\in J_i} q_j = \overline{q}_i$. The production process consists of a sequence of *main production* steps and each job family requires a subsequence of this, i.e., all jobs of the same job family have to go through the same production steps. Each J_i has *routing alternatives* $R_i^1,\dots R_i^{a_i}$, where each R_i^l is a sequence of stages, each *stage* being a subsequence of steps. The stages of each routing alternative must be disjointed and their union must give the set of steps required by J_i. With each stage s, there is associated a set of machines M_i^s. The *processing time* of job $j\in J_i$ on some machine $M_k \in M_i^s$ is defined as $p_{j,k} = q_j / v_i^k$, where v_i^k is the *yield* of M_k (items/time unit) when processing any job of J_i. Each machine M_k has a *calendar* specifying those time periods when the machine is available for processing. There are *sequence dependent setup times* between the jobs of different job families scheduled on the same machine. Let $u_k(j_1,j_2)$ denote the setup time between the jobs j_1,j_2 on M_k. It is 0 if jobs j_1 and j_2 belong to the same job family and $u_k(j_1,j_2) = u_k(j_3,j_4)$ whenever $j_1,j_3 \in J_{i1}$ and $j_2,j_4 \in J_{i2}$ for some i_1 and i_2.

Assumption 1. In the following a (job, stage) pair (j, s) will be called *operation*. If a machine becomes unavailable during the processing of an operation or setup, then the processing stops and resumes immediately once the machines become available again. However, setups and operations cannot be interrupted for any other reason.

A *solution* to our problem is a triple (ρ,μ,π) with the following content:

- ρ is a selection of routing alternatives. That is, $\rho(i)\in\{1,\dots,a(i)\}$ specifies exactly one route for J_1, and all jobs of the same job family will use the same route.
- μ is a selection of machines. For each job $j\in J_i$, and each stage $s\in R_i^{p(i)}$, μ(j, s) is a machine from M_i^s. Distinct jobs of the same job family may be performed on different machines.
- π is a permutation of operations on the machines. Namely, π_k is a permutation of those operations that are assigned to machine M_k by μ.

Drótos, Erdős, Kis, March, 2007, ch. 3. the scheduling problem, p. 4-6.

2.1. The Game of Life and the Turing Machine

The Game of Life was invented by Princeton mathematician, John Conway, published by Scientific American's Mathematical Games section, in October 1970. It consists of a collection of cells on a plane, which, based on a few mathematical rules, can live, die or multiply. It is based on von Neumann's idea about the possibility of a self-organizing machine structure by a cellular computer, and can realize programmable tasks solvable on a universal Turing machine.

Epistemologically, it is a convincing demonstration of the universality of the Turing concept and by that of the universally emerging development of any mathematically, computer-materializable model.

On the Game of Life infinite grid the cells can have live or dead states with the following rules:

1. Any live cell with fewer than two live neighbors dies, as if by under population.
2. Any live cell with more than three live neighbors dies, as if by overcrowding.
3. Any live cell with two or three live neighbors lives, unchanged, to the next generation.
4. Any tile with exactly three live neighbors cells will be populated with a living cell.

Illustration of the rules of Conway's game of the life

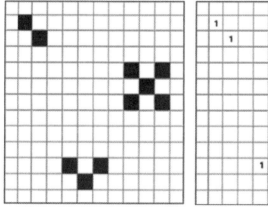 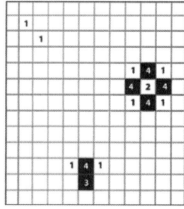

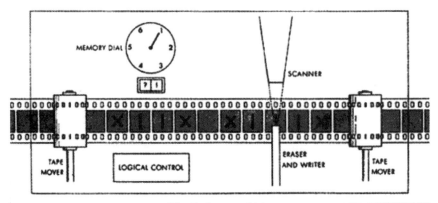

The Turing machine

One iteration in Conway's Game of Life. Little animals 1 die from loneliness. Little animals 2 die from overspill population. Little animals 3 survive. Little animals 4 procreate.

The obvious question: can the Game of Life or any similar system of a few basic components and rules generate such complex entities as the human being? The answer of physics for all kind of elements and molecules built from them is a theoretically and experimentally well proven fact. This is also true for the evolutionary line of life. The link between the two seems to be a similar problem of research. The latter statement is not yet proven, nevertheless current knowledge on molecular biology and further evolution is a sufficient background for our considerations about the developmental procedures of modeling, computations and, first of all, about the epistemic problems of right choices in these basically mental abstraction processes. The philosophical thinking of von Neumann and Turing, not to speak about others, concentrate on this statement and its deep, farsighted consequences.

The Turing machine, first published by Alan Turing in 1936, much before the ideas and technology of the modern computer, is a similar thought experiment of starting with some very basic components and rules. A machine that can do only four simplest operations of two kinds: step forward and back, read or write one type of symbol (symbol or void). The machine operates the memory-instruction medium: an infinite tape with individual cells for the individual signs. A reminder: the most complex and sophisticated software-driven computer systems are not more and not less than evolutionary products of this simple ideal just like our body emerged from the simplest protozoa!

An *operation example* of the Turing machine, how with unary numbers, 4 and 2, a subtraction operation is executed on and with the endless tape of the machine.

Turing machine operation

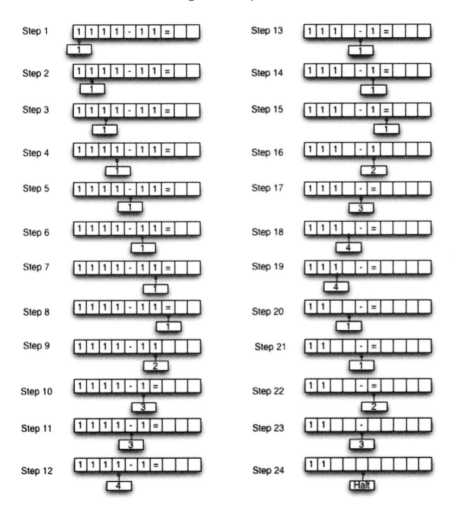

2.2. History of notations

By relieving the mind of all unnecessary work, a good notation sets it free to concentrate on more advanced problems, and in effect increases the mental power of the race.
Alfred North Whitehead

Notation of algebraic operations did not follow the course of notation of numbers. The conceptual world of operations is much more subtle and required a new era of calculus sophistication.

In prehistory, the Egyptians, having symbols as a writing practice, used the hieroglyphs of two legs for addition and subtraction, the one going forward, the other going back. Euclid, in the culmination of Greek geometry, used extensively literal notations for definitions and proofs, what for they considered to be useful, without the intention of using more general operation symbols.

Diophantos of Alexandria, who probably lived in the third century CE, used some kind of notations for his still remarkable study in algebraic equations, but it was too clumsy for further application and the historic decline of the Antiquity closed any continuation.

Experts in the Hindu-Arabic culture find some traces of notational thinking, but the real development in the late fourteenth and specially in the fifteenth and sixteenth century with the great progress of calculations in physics. Before that, arithmetic operations were marked by simple juxtapositions and some two-dimensional tables (especially in China), just for notes of intermediate calculation results.

After early application of signs for addition and subtraction, used as abbreviations, and some other non-systematical notations, the French François Viète, (1540–1603), an amateur mathematician and astronomer, developed the first methodical design. Viète, as many of his age, was a public personality involved in the messy politics of the period, and the periods of being dismissed gave him and others the opportunity to sacrifice his talents for science. He was also a practicing cryptographer. At the court of Henry IV he managed to break a Spanish secret cipher.

Viète influenced many people, because of the general scientific revolution in physics and first of all, in astronomy, a science stimulating the mechanics of earthly dynamics. One of them was the English William Oughtred (1574-1660), the inventor of the slide rule and author of a relevant book on mathematics, that was read by Isaac Newton (1642-1727). The data are here important, to see the context of notation, calculus, astronomy, and dynamics. The parallel story of philosophy and theology belongs to another study.

Oughtred's French contemporary was René Descartes (1596-1650) who, renewing the connection of mathematics with geometry, added far reaching issues to the notation custom.

The early development of notations in Italy found followers in German countries, e.g., the astronomer Johann Müller Regiomontanus (1436-1476) and others, but the real step forward was marked by Gottfried Willhelm Leibniz (1646-1716), a contemporary of Newton, who was born only four years earlier but died eleven years later. They created the instruments of mathematical physics, infinitesimal calculus, and algebraic continuation of arithmetics to the realm of dynamics, realized in resolution and summation with small linear steps. Leibniz was the first thinker of notational logic, preparing a centuries-long sequence of expressing all phenomena in the form of logical constructions, the great endeavor towards the Frege, Hilbert, and Russell program.

In the literature we find different names: the first to use x for an unknown, indefinite value; the dot for multiplication; the colon for division; what were the first literal notations for constants, variables, functions, operations. These names changed depending on the author, mostly related to the mentioned masters and schools. For us, the evolutionary process was more interesting, why did the coincidence of necessities and ideas arise, the need for fertile social soils for orientation of great minds who are always present but effective only in certain given conditions? The Mark Twain story of Captain Stromfield returns in positive and negative morals. (Captain Stromfield visiting Heaven was looking for the greatest strategist of history. He was introduced to a provincial cobbler who, in spite his extraordinary talents, had no opportunity to develop them on the earth.)

In spite of all these developments, there still exist several schools of mathematics preferring different notation styles, not against the general progress of science.

2.3. The Development of Algebra

The development of algebra was connected with the history of using numbers and notations. The level of abstraction was motivated by the necessities and conceptual forms of these applications. The partly independent line of number mysticism, present in all early civilizations, and for us best represented by Pythagoras, was a beautiful mind game but had its limits, as in nature's way of abstraction. Our favorite Game of Life is a very modern idea and has only slender connections with the earlier phantasms. This connection is treated in more details in speaking about hidden patterns of mind in their intuitive association roles.

People, meeting calculation tasks, soon developed some general methods for solving similar problems. All early civilizations were confronted with such problems in construction, calendar design, moving armies, distributing goods, and therefore we find some more or less algebraic-type, rather sophisticated calculation rules in the early Egyptian, Mesopotamian, Indian, Chinese, and even American civilizations. The three and a half millennia old documents, papyri, e.g., the best-known *Rhind papyrus*, and tablets refer to even older origins.

The development of algebra was closely connected to the development of number concepts. What was first deeply considered was the abstracted meanings of natural numbers and their rational fractions, and much later in Indian mathematics, negative numbers by Brahmagupta after 600 CE, and further, the concept of zero and roots of quadratic equations by Bhaskara after 800 CE.

The emergence of more abstracted, i.e. more general concepts, were born only by the combined maturing of general conceptual thinking and application needs. This is the reason why the nearly modern Greek logical rigor, expressed in the geometry of Euclid (working around 300 BCE) was not present in algebraic works. Even the most advanced trends of Greek algebra, summarized by *Diophantos of Alexandria*, about 500 years after Euclid, could not perform at the level of the Euclidean geometry, though he seems to be the first conscious thinker about notation, being the next relevant step in the algebraic conceptual world.

The other, somehow separated, development was related to notation. This is the reason why it is separately treated here.

The great period of modern algebra is closely bound to the world views of modern science which dramatically extended the world view from the natural limitations of human sensory and communication confinement.

The lesson is interesting: though fantasy had no objective limits, nor was inhibited by any professional scientific rigor, the creation of far working abstractions was earthbound. Two- and three-dimensional, roaming in linear spaces and times of human measures outlined the domain of thinking, mostly even in fiction.

Our epistemic devotion to the role of modern algebra is rooted in this conceptual liberation of mind. Modern geometry-related algebra provides a spaceship from the outlined limitations of perception, and, remarkably, the mental spaceship is built from earthly material. This earthly material is the axiomatic conceptual system stemming from the primitive arithmetic, the starting components of the Game of Life and the Turing machine.

The flourishing of this relieved thinking started with the general revolution of science and human relations at about the turn of the 18th and 19th centuries and is not completed until now due to new opportunities in science, especially in physics. We can refer here to really motivating and highly authentic literature (Hawking, Penrose, Shafarevich, van der Waerden).

2.4. The Evolution of Number Concepts and their Combined Algebraic-Physical Representation.

The evolution of the number concept is a trace of development in coordinatization of more and more complex phenomena. This joins the great question of the universal continuity of the phenomena interpreted by physics and consequently, the continuities between physics, chemistry, biology, biological phenomena, and the human mind. The final answer about the developmental continuity should be the complete artificial reproduction proof, foreseen by Feynman and now Venter and, by many others before and after.

From our more modest perspective this means the algebraic continuity of calculus, modeling and computer representation. This is not equivalent to the final answer but it is a singular flash on the real problem, just due to its possibilities and limitations.

The essential limitation is, of course, the complexity/non-computability barrier, though it cannot be a final proof against the general continuity model.

The non-computability barrier is a hard obstacle of any complete reconstruction proof, first of all, of the cybernetic dream of an artificial human mind equipped with all capabilities of a living creature. How hard this barrier is, concerning all unforeseen developments of computational algorithmics and mechanisms, is on the one hand the subject of fiction, alien from this essay, and on the other, a recurrent item in the course of this presentation, regarding some emerging perspectives of non-conventional, new developments and their epistemic lessons. In this view the model is more than a metaphor of realizability.

The continuity of the number concept is represented by their inclusive hierarchy (below)

$\mathbb{N} \subseteq \mathbb{Z} \subseteq \mathbb{Q} \subseteq \mathbb{R} \subseteq \mathbb{C}$, where

$\mathbb{N}$ (Natural numbers), positive integers, with **0**,

$\mathbb{Z}$ (Zahlen) denotes the positive and negative integers,

$\mathbb{Q}$ (Quotient) the rational numbers composed by fractions by elements of $\mathbb{Z}$,

$\mathbb{R}$ (Real) numbers, rational and irrational numbers, possibly with an infinite decimal representation,

$\mathbb{C}$ (Complex) numbers.

All basic algebraic operations (addition to division) can be deduced from simple individual counting or counting down with the units: one + one…. – one… and so on. These individual, unique steps comply with the individual operations of the Game of Life or of the Turing machine. The problem can be continued with the linear case of infinitely small individual steps (infinitely to any small unity) in a process of linear progress in infinitesimal calculi. The fact is well applied in solving differential equations with the analogous algebraic characteristic equations.

An entirely different method, a passage to the limit, gives the real numbers $\mathbb{R}$, on an infinite line, and then again an algebraic construction yields the complex numbers $\mathbb{C}$, coordinatization on a surface. The *Hamiltonian quaternions*, $\mathbb{H}$, have no commutative multiplication, unlike the preceding types of numbers.

This means the omission of the commutativity condition: ab ≠ ba. The consequences of counting and counting down, i.e.. the consequences of reversal operations, predictions from previous progress are ambivalent. The same consequence is continued in the infinitesimal case, especially important in the Lie group, Hamiltonian operator calculations, in the fundamental equations of physical and other transformations. The meaning of these non- commutative operations refers to the further problem of process reversibility.

The other group quality is the *associativity*, a reference to the linear or nonlinear nature of counting increments. In any problem of modeling, the linear hypothesis within reasonable limits is essential, we apply either linear approximations or break up the model into quasilinear sections. The original model should be extended by some further rules of combinational growth (the exponential and logarithmic algorithms) and rules of growth and decay limits, hopefully reducible to the above balance conditions. Developments can be modeled by polynomial approximations which fit into the extended simple scheme.

Here we return to our perspective of operation-rule continuity: Can a more complex model be reduced automatically to the original operations of the Beginnings? The extension of the individual stepwise counting reaches the model complexity of the polynomials. The counting down is ambivalent with real and complex roots, some having a well definable meaning and interpretation by physical quantities. Other roots were or are not yet defined by trivial looking physical existence-interpretations and they can lead into another world of virtual reality. Virtual reality in this sense does not mean the popular multimedia applications but a world of phenomena not deducible from the origins in a direct way.

The problem of the roots and interpretations of polynomials led *Galois* to the algebraic *group* concept.

The algebraic homologies can cover factual, physical or other relations, suggestions about non-accidental coincidences. The deep epistemic meaning of this concept is the continuous deduction possibility among different worlds of phenomena. This is the problem of different or continuously evolving nature of computational-modeling operations.

How different these lessons and sometimes vague ideas are, two frequently cited quotations are selected from this multitude:

– Dedekind: numbers are free creations of the human mind; they serve as a means of apprehending more easily and more sharply the difference of things. It is only through building up the science of numbers and thus acquiring the continuous number-domain that we are prepared to accurately investigate our notions of space and time by bringing them into relation with this number-domain created in our mind (1887).

– Kronecker: God made the integers, all the rest is man's work (1886).

These are continued in the philosophical considerations of recent great thinkers of physics and mathematics, e.g., Hawking, Penrose, and Chaitin.

If we consider the Riemannian extension of the Euclidean geometry, i. e., the aspect of spaces and dimensions, the smooth transition of operations can be accepted and applied. This smooth transition refers to the way of thinking in model extension, and as current hypotheses of cosmology demonstrate, probably to physical reality, as well.

2.5. A Simplified Review of Some Basic Algebraic Concepts, Operations and Axioms

A *field* is a set with two binary operations (addition, multiplication) satisfying the following axioms:

> *addition:*
> commutativity: a+b = b+a
> associativity: a+(b+c) = (a+b)+c
> existence of a zero element: a+0 = a
> negative element: a, -a; a-a = 0 (additive inverse)
> *multiplication:*
> commutativity: ab = ba
> associativity: a(bc) = (ab)c

existence of an identity element: 1, a.1 = a
existence of an inverse element: a⁻¹; a.a⁻¹ = 1 if a ≠ 0
addition and multiplication:
distributivity: a(b+c) = ab+ac
e.g., rational, real and complex numbers

A *commutative ring* is the same as the field with the exception of multi-plicative inverses, e.g., integers and integer-valued functions on a set.

A *group* is a set of elements with a binary operation, multiplica-tive, notation: o which is associative, has an identity element **1,** and every element **a** has an inverse **a⁻¹** such that **aoa⁻¹ = a⁻¹oa.**

A basic example of a finite group is the *symmetric group*, which is the group of *permutations* of a set of objects. The simplest infinite group is the set of *integers* under usual addition. For continuous groups, one can consider the real numbers or the set of *invertible matrices*. These two are examples of *Lie groups*.

A *morphism* is a map between similar algebraic objects (such as groups) which commute with the operations. For example, a group homomorphism j stratifies:

$$\varphi(a \circ b) = \varphi(a) \circ \varphi(b)$$

Perhaps the most important kind of morphism is *isomorphism*, which is *bijective, invertible* morphism whose inverse is also a morphism.

The graph isomorphism as an example:

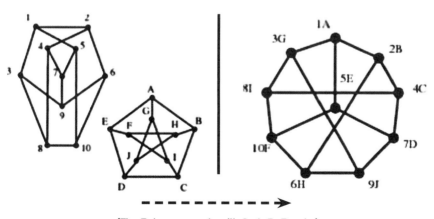

(The Petersen graph, with 1–A, 2–B... etc.)

2.6. Support Vector, Simulated Annealing, Markovian Chains, Monte Carlo Methods

Support vector method is a widely used procedure for discrimination of features of a set, i.e., for the general pattern-recognition problem. For discrimination of two features, e.g., patients with a fever and normal temperature, we try to find a discriminating plane on the map of the patients' body temperature. If further data are also required for diagnostic decision, the discriminating plane should be a multidimensional surface of one dimension less than the number of features. Finding such planes is an optimization method for distances between the surface and the feature points. By that we get the support vectors of discrimination surfaces. Projection of this discriminating surface on the individual feature plane, i.e., application of kernel computation is the second part of the feature extraction. The combination of this surface finding optimization that can also be a statistical operation and the kernel projection was the achievement of Vapnik (1971, 1998).

Simulated annealing is an optimization approximation method based on the slow annealing process of improving and equalizing

Support vector

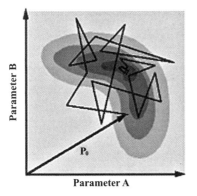 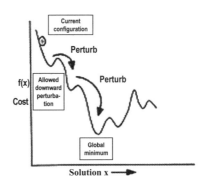

Simulated annealing

metallic materials. The metal is heated and slowly cooled, allowing the molecules to move toward more uniform tempered states, with less strain and more free crystallizing. In the optimization task, the feature to be optimized is the analogy of the energy (mostly represented by temperature), the cautious cooling is the search for this energy gradient with respect to the neighboring points in the space of the problem. This stepwise approximation provides the picture of worse and better regions, and clarifies the realizable optimal or suboptimal compromise solutions.

Markovian chains are stochastic, random processes in which, given the present state, the future states are independent of the past of the system. Classical random walk is an example. The chain represents the independence or dependence of information from another one. The state transitions have certain probabilities and the process is supposed to be stationary.

The hidden Markovian methods attempt to discover unapparent Markovian-relations within great amount of data.

Markov-chain

Monte Carlo method

Monte Carlo methods are a wide class of computational methods which make substantial use of (pseudo)sampling. They are used when deterministic methods are not sufficient. Monte Carlo techniques turned out to be particularly useful in simulating complex systems.

The randomness, i.e. the avoidance of any bias, prejudice in the search procedure is mostly warranted by random numbers. These can be generated by basically random physical phenomena or by special pseudorandom computer algorithms.

2.7. Lie Algebra and Group

Lie groups represent all kinds of smooth transformations, those computable with linear and quasi-linear differential expressions. This means that all physical, biological and social phenomena that are continuous in a region and/or in a time period or can be approximated in that way, are usually treated with Lie-group representations. Rotations around a symmetry axis, translations, reflections, displacements, and linear distortions, are the typical transformations. Combined expressions and linear differential matrices are the instruments of computation with Lie groups. Due to the representation of symmetry, all kinds of dynamic balances—and with the Poisson-Lie bracket expressions—lack of balances, and the search for undiscovered, omitted balancing components can be followed. This is the reason

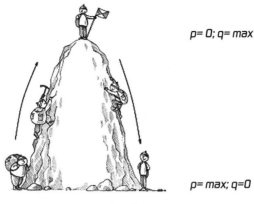

p= 0; q= max

p= max; q=0

Hamiltonian

why fundamental transformation-dynamic balance equations, e.g., the Hamiltonians of mechanical and analogous dynamics, quantum dynamics included, and the Maxwell equations of electrodynamics, are all represented by Lie groups and calculated by Lie algebras.

The Hamiltonian dynamics in Lie algebra terms:
notation:
H= T+V, the sum of the kinetic and potential energy,
p= momenta
q= generalized coordinates (translational, rotational)

The figure represents a terribly simplified picture of the Hamiltonian motion- energy relations where:

$$\frac{\mathrm{d}}{\mathrm{d}t}q(t) = \frac{\partial}{\partial p}H\big(p(t),q(t),t\big)$$

expresses the changes of a system regarding its temporal, local (coordinates) and motion (momentum) as a function of the H (energy) relations.

The balances are represented by the *Poisson (Lie)-brackets*, the difference of the H (energy) relations:

$$\frac{\partial H}{\partial p} - \frac{\partial H}{\partial q} = \big[\mathbf{H}_\mathrm{p},\mathbf{H}_\mathrm{q}\big]$$

The expressions and the dimensions of the metric are simplified for the illustration of the symmetries and analogies.

The difference is zero if the described transitions are perfect, but this is usually not the case, something remains as the quantity of other phenomena, being hidden or lost. Here, we find a physical meaning of differences between commutative and non-commutative algebras! The search for these unbalances led to the most important discoveries of modern physics, the latest being the search for a missing member of the standard particle model and the mysterious presence of black holes and the gravitational material of cosmology.

The theory of *Lie groups* and related algebras is now a singular instrument of mathematics and theoretical physics. Lie groups provide a solid theoretical basis for the study of smoothly changing symmetries, having an especially relevant role when studying geometrical properties of nonlinear differential equations modeling physical phenomena. Lie algebras are local tools to work with these symmetries. The physical transformations can occur smoothly, with infinitely small steps, and others in discrete steps, defining gauges and certain distances of the permissible states.

The simple examples of mechanical transformations in the *Hamiltonian Lie groups* are typical in the three dimensional smooth transformation groups. Another relevant feature of these group transformations is the preservation of relevant invariants, in physics in general, of energy and impulse.

The Maxwell-equations

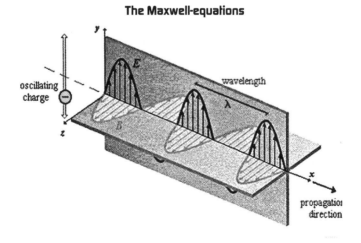

Beyond the realm of motion, the other general world of phenomena is modeled by the Maxwellian equations of electrodynamics. This world is usually described by means of vector algebra but is basically identical to the Hamiltonian concept. The Hamiltonian, i.e., the generalized energy represents the electrical and magnetic potentials and the mechanical energy creating and created by the interactions of these potential fields. The transformations between the three and the dynamics of these are natural parallels of the motion equations, expressed in partial differentials of time and space. The reason why this Hamiltonian portrayal is not used, is the visual and computational elegance and simplicity of the vector representation. The essential similarity can be seen after a glance at a simple form of the basic Maxwell equations:

$$curl\,E = -\frac{\partial B}{\partial t} \qquad curl\,B = \alpha I + \beta\frac{\partial B}{\partial t}$$

where *curl* is the rotational differential operator, for location related differential changes in orthogonal direction of a surface, a kernel type algebraic operation,

B= magnetic field, magnetic flux density, Volt.sec

E=electrical field, Volt/meter,

α, β are usually constants, depending on the medium and metric,

I = density of electrical current Volt/meter square.

Coordinated transformations

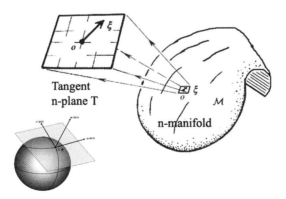

The visual representation is instructive for receiving an impression of the orthogonal electrical and magnetic fields with the current direction

The metaphor of motion is represented by vectors—vector differential equations creating vector fields of permissible trajectories, and tangent vectors as associated orbits of motion—describing the course of various processes.

3.1. Basic notations

NOTATION FOR PROPOSITIONAL LOGIC

P, Q, A, B,... are propositions, statements being true or false
(T and F, resp. 1 and 0 denoting the logical values)
($\neg$P) for not P
(P $\vee$ Q) for P or Q
(P $\wedge$ Q) for P and Q
(P => Q) for P implies Q
(P iff Q) for P if and only if Q

NOTATION FOR QUANTIFIERS AND PREDICATE LOGIC

$\exists x$ there is a P
$\forall x$ for all P

SYLLOGISMS

Categorical syllogism: If A is in C then B is in C.
Disjunctive syllogism: If A is true, then B is false (A or B).
Conditional syllogism: If A is true then B is true (If A then B).
Modus Ponens: If X is true then Y is true. X is true. Therefore Y is true.
Modus Tollens: If X is true then Y is true. Y is false. Therefore X is false.

All further syllogistic formulae concerning implications for triplets and further predicates (true or false statements) are combinations of the above syllogistic primitives and *nothing more*.

This statement was heavily discussed during the drafting of this text. References were made to hardly resolvable embedded structures of higher order logic and other refinements, especially for uncertain conditionals. The sentence remained as it is, I couldn't find any publications which provide a firm proof against the statement and cannot be resolved to the enumerated primitives, finally to the logical operations of the Turing model.

The above summary of notations and basic syllogisms doesn't claim for any textbook completeness or usually required mathematical, logical precision. It is a small reminder of the simple logical instruments which are applied in programming in a direct or indirect way, and is a reference to the essential epistemic statement.

Clause is a group of words containing a subject and a predicate and functioning as a member of a complex or compound sentence. *Program A runs*, this is a clause with *program, A, and run*.

A *Horn clause* is a disjunction of symbols and words, with at most one positive, i.e., having the logical value: true. This expresses in a closed world of statements an exclusive explication of the only positive.

In the world of a family composed of girls, boys, grandma, mother, and father, the definition of the father by a Horn clause:

$$father \Rightarrow \neg\, girls \Rightarrow \neg\, boys \lor \neg\, grandma \lor \neg\, mother$$

Horn-clause

This family create a closed world of the indicated family member symbols and the father is the positive member of this world in the closed respect of being male and neither female nor child. All these feature conditions must be and can be logically defined before.

3.2. Non-Monotonic Logic

In a system of an open world not all statements corroborate the previous ones under every condition. Hypotheses or conclusions which are logical antecedents or consequences of these statements are uncertain due to influences of the open world, outside of the world of discussion. Monotonic logic is created in a closed world where all further statements, data, and facts add to the validity of the previous ones.

Non-monotonic logic looks at these contradictory states of statements and attempts to find a consistent way of resolving the situation by adding further new conditions or canceling some old ones.

In classical logic all theorems are results of valid inferences, in non-monotonic logic one starts with all inferred statements, whether they are consistent or not. Then in most cases one starts to find a fixed point, i.e., a minimal set where all statements get a consistent context. *Birds include all warm-blooded, egg-laying, feathered vertebrates with forelimbs modified to form wings*, this is a general extended class for birds, and for Europeans *wings are used for flying*, for Australians, this latter should be excluded from the definition conditions because *some birds don't fly*.

Several methods were developed for restoring consistency, e.g., *circumscription, default, autoepistemic logic, Truth Maintenance Systems*.

CIRCUMSCRIPTION

"We know some objects in a given class and we have some ways of generating more. We jump to the conclusion that this gives all the objects in the class. Thus we *circumscribe* the class to the objects we know how to generate."

"It is only a conjecture, because there might be an object such that" a predicate on the object "is not generated in this way." "The heuristics of circumscription—when one can plausibly conjecture that the objects generated in known ways are all there are—are completely unstudied."

Circumscription is not deduction in disguise, because every form of deduction has two properties that circumscription lacks—transitivity and what we may call monotonicity. Transitivity says that "if *a* is a consequence of *b* and *c* is a consequence of *b*, then *c* is a consequence of *a*." (If snowing, the road is slippery, if slippery then driving is dangerous, consequently if snowing then driving is dangerous.) In realistic cases (circumscription) driving on snow by a car equipped with tire chains is not dangerous. *Monotonicity* says that within a class of statements all further sentences corroborate the statement further. No exception or contradiction occurs. This is not the case in circumscription and generally in *non-monotonic logic* because we find some exceptional cases, e.g., the penguin is a bird which does not fly. The way of circumventing this difficulty is to find a minimum model where all sentences are true (e.g., European birds, cars with standard, low mileage tires, etc.). Nevertheless "It is not always true that a sentence true in all minimal models can be proved by circumscription. Indeed, the minimal model of *Peano's axiom* is the standard model of arithmetic and Gödel's theorem is the assertion that not all true sentences are theorems. Minimal models don't always exist, and when they exist, they are not always unique." [1]

DEFAULT LOGIC

This is a method (Reiter 1980) for treating non-monotonic problems. The basic idea is a distinction between general "hard" rules (facts) and their defaults, i.e., those rules which extend the world of the facts by exemptions and irregularities. (All birds fly but penguins do not.) The method is similar to circumscription, the main difference is the theoretically well-formed idea of circumscription's minimal set, related to the fixed point theorems. A weakness of default logic is the arbitrary and occasional nature of the default rules. They cannot be inferred within the system, they can be used for further inference with much caution, and they can yield trivial contradictions.

---

[1] The quotations are from *McCarthy* (1977), the logical formulae are substituted by verbal explanation and examples.

Autoepistemic logic

Autoepistemic logic (Stalnaker, 1980; Moore, 1985) is a typical conceptual frame of a closed world. It contains a set of beliefs of an agent and a language that can generate this kind of a closed world. The hierarchical version takes a set of those that can interact but they are closed in the set of these individual subsets.

In spite of its closeness requirement this logic is non-monotonic as well, the language can generate nonsense or contradictions from a valid set of beliefs–there is no protection for machines, neither for people!

Counterfactuals

This is a logic based on negative, excluding statements. For example: *If it's not a brain injury, it would be Alzheimer disease.* The logical implications are therefore different from regular syllogisms, nevertheless, several of the Aristotelian schemes fully cover the concept, moreover it is (was!) extended to possibilistic modalities as well. It is related to non-monotonic logic and naturally to the different worlds concept (Ginsberg, 1986).

Truth Maintenance Systems (TMS)

The original idea of Doyle in 1979 was an establishment of a bridge between monotonic and non-monotonic cases. In a monotonic case we have an antecedent precondition, e.g., *It is raining,* and logical consequence *we get wet.* TMS adds assumptions to this (*if we do not take an umbrella, if we go out early, if we cannot walk under the arcade,* etc.). The program maintains the knowledge base of the reasoner. The system checks the truth of the precondition-consequence relations but it does the same for the assumptions, especially if the logical procedure starts to be non-monotonic (*we get wet → get a cold → miss the performance*). The TMS revises the assumptions to restore the consistency and informs the reasoner about the process. The relation with the Dempster-Shafer uncertainty estimation method is just the consideration of a group of conditions, a difference between them may occur if certain evidences are (or can be) added to these groups and the situations are not simply binary ones.

The *ATMS* (Assumption-Based Truth Maintenance Systems, de Kleer, 1986) is a further development of the same idea, calling the set of assumptions an environment and reducing this to a minimal set as is done by circumscription. The closed-world assumption is maintained by this procedure and, detecting a conflict, the system checks the assumptions until it can return to the monotonic situation.

The non-monotonic nature of a discourse is illustrated by paradoxes as parables.

3.3. Quantum Computation

Quantum computation is a research field for application of the quantum-theoretical states and properties of particle physics. Such properties and phenomena include the spin of various particles, and such features of the theory as superposition and entanglement. A two bit classical computer memory can be in one of the 2^n possible states at a given time of computation. A quantum-computer operating on n qubits is in a superposition of all the 2^n states. As an example, for a 300-qubit quantum register, somewhere on the order of $2^{300} = 10^{90}$ classical registers are required, more than there are atoms in the observable universe. This immense representational and theoretical computational power could solve those computationally inaccessible problems where extremely high numbers of successive operations and checks are required, e.g., factoring numbers into a product of primes, code breaking, etc.

The major problem is the reading of these representations due to the state change and the statistical nature of the quantum phenomena. Several theoretical and experimental efforts try to overcome these using special optical effects, extremely low temperature, high vacuum particle traps, other quantum phenomena related to special carbon phases (*graphene*), etc. For the time being, practical applications are a long way off.

Many algorithms are constructed for an ideal quantum computer and they stimulate further instruments for problem solving with other advanced hardware. A prominent example is *Shor's algorithm* for factoring integers on a hypothetical quantum computer in polyno-mial time. No such fast method is known to exist on traditional com-puters. Shor's method opens up the possibility, that some computa-tional problems can be solved much faster on quantum computers than on classical ones.

Grover's algorithm is a *quantum algorithm* for searching an un-sorted database with *N* entries in $O(N^{1/2})$ time and using $O(\log N)$ storage space.

3.4. Prolog, Logic Programming

PROLOG is, on the one hand, a user-friendly language for writing programs in first-order logic, i.e., setting predicates and names of a priori defined objects and writing logical relations for and to them, as well as statements about the truth values and relations among the predicates. These relations are the classic minimal set of first-order logic extended by quantifiers (*for all*, *exists*) and variables, defining the predicates. The variables permit to define some basic arithmetic relations (*less than, more or equal to*), and it is an easy support for a primitive linguistic dialogue.

The first further step is the automatic transcription to *Horn claus-es* for an easy automation of the resolution principle, i.e., resolving the set of logical sentences by proving that the negative of the state-ment leads to a false expression. It is clear that, starting a program, the designer should give fixed statements about the items to work with, e.g., the name of a work piece: ball, all its relevant properties: iron, round, clean, all the conditions of working with: clean: yes, iron: no, and so on, similarly for a disease, an economic situation, or anything. The program cannot say more, investigating the condi-tions and their logical consequence, the operation is possible or not. The operation itself, e.g., finishing, opening the heart, investing in a power service, requires the logical sequence in an analogous order, using some calculations about the surface behavior, the blood circu-lation, or the behavior of the stock exchange. These most relevant parts of the program are not different from any other similar task, us-ing prefab mathematical computations, patterns of similar cases, discovering such similarities, i.e., using in part the available professional experience of other experts or of their own.

Several further structural programming simplifications–creating hierarchies of statements about truth or false consequences, naming, definition of further abstractions–can be added to consolidate certain knowledge. The knowledge itself stands beyond and not in the logic programming, and that is the main lesson for us, the window for limits of knowledge.

3.5. Paradoxes, Undecidability

The paradox of undecidable statements has many witty variants from Antiquity to the present. (Protagoras, Epimenides, Eubulides, Russell, Smullyan, etc.) These are the prototypical parables cautioning against a belief in overall truth validity of logic reasoning.

The ancient problems of paradoxes started to be renewed for modern logic after the revolutionary ideas of Cantor: Does the set of all sets exist or not? The famous *Russell-paradox* is a nice example: *A barber declares that he is shaving all and only those people who do not shave themselves. But what about the barber himself?*

These questions led to *Gödel's theorem* in 1931, which may be considered one of the most important innovations in logical aspects of epistemology since the Greeks, and treated somewhat more detail here. No really closed world exists. System based on axioms can generate a theorem which cannot be proved within the framework of the referenced axiomatic world. More precisely: In a (sufficiently rich) theory–theory being understood in the precise mathematical sense– one can always formulate a theorem whose truth or validity cannot be proved in the system. Tasks which are not solvable within the framework of the task were found by Church (1936) and others. The *halting problem* (Turing, 1936) is a nice illustration: It was proven that there does not exist any *general* program which can decide if another program ever halts or not, for any legal input of the program.

The *Russell paradox* is, in some sense, a reformulation of one of the oldest: the *Cretan Liar*, who points at all other Cretans, declares that all Cretans are liars.

The Cretan Liar

The Cretan Liar gained a new timeliness in computer systems as the problem of self-reference. In a closed system, as in a society where everybody is a consistent liar, the relations of truth and falsity are unambiguous, equivalent to a society of consistently veracious people. In some Bulgarian cultures, for example, the ways of nodding for yes or no are opposite to the European habit, and their communication is unambiguous, if they do not meet people of other cultures. Problems start if the two systems meet along a border that implies a self-reference. (as with *Russell's barber*, who is part of the barber system himself, there could be a group of such barbers). We see how the different worlds' idea is related to the self-reference problem: Different worlds can have different references and a conflict starts at any intersection of the two worlds. This has been the reason for most of mankind's conflicts and is now a renewed phenomenon in every system of independent (or independently designed) components. The *Liar's paradox*, the *Russell paradox* and the paradoxes of different worlds appear in our computerized systems as interface problems with interfacing programs, program components and interconnections with physical systems.

We can also find an uncertainty variant of the Liar's paradox among the four types of *Eubulides paradoxes*. This is the *Hooded* story: "You state that you know your brother. But the man who came around and his face was covered, was your brother and you did not recognize him" (*Lucianus: Bión Praxis*, 22). Translated to our problems, this story means an uncertain reference taken as certain because it was received from a generally reliable source. This situation is rapidly spreading; the amount of knowledge which should be used in every single task is unmanageable and sources cannot be checked. Knowledge-based systems start to provide these as a real-time service (e.g., an EKG or EEG analysis)–the basis of the knowledge base is hooded! The original metaphor was used for an incomplete reference description but, as we discussed earlier, such an interpretation does not differ from our views on uncertainty.

A slightly different paradox of *Eubulides*, the *Horned*, is related to the reference problem as well: "What you have not lost, you have it. But you have not lost horns, i.e., you still have horns." (Diogenes Laertius, lib. VII, 187). These kinds of references are problems for temporal logic and the closed world assumption. At each instance, we meet such surprises, which are trivial for a pragmatic human actor equipped with broad tacit knowledge, but are paradoxes, sources of deadlocks and contradictions for artificial systems that rely only on programmed information. By a further generalization, we return to the different worlds idea. A programmed machine world meets a real one, equipped with all kinds of facts (knowledge) that were not considered for the machine world.

The antique paradoxes of The Bold or the Heap about the uncertain limits of definitions, how much hair or sand should define the

The Bold or the Heap

beginning of being bald or of naming a surface heap, are the paradoxes of the later fuzzy concepts.

Modern-time paradoxes relate to the uncertainty viewed from different points of views, different persons of the same situation. They are descendants of the *Hooded paradox*.

In *The Tree Prisoners Paradox* one of the prisoners is sentenced, the two others will be freed, but they don't know the final verdict. One of them receives information that increases his subjective expectation of being sentenced from one in two. The fact that each one has a chance of one in three was not changed by that. According to the *Ace of Spades* paradox any card in a deck of 52 has a probability of 1/52 from the observation perspective, the probability of the ace's appearance is either 0 or 1.

Typical paradoxes about the non-monotonicity of logic reasoning are the birds, such as the *penguin* which don't fly, and many others. The consequence is contradictory if we do not permit exceptions in the flow of logic or some probabilistic distribution of the two

Penguin, the bird which does not fly

different consequences, forgetting to think about the closed world assumptions.

The other quoted paradox is *the Yale Shooting Problem*. A gun is loaded at a given time and the gun is fired (at Fred) at another time. How can we conclude that Fred is dead or alive? The problem is dependent on the temporal processes: what is the sequence of events? Is the gun in-between somehow unloaded or not? The *Yale Shooting Problem* is a paradigm for temporal logic and temporal projections (Hanks and McDermott 1986).

(Nevertheless, *Goethe: Reduction of the effect to the cause is only a historical procedure, e.g., the effect of a man killed to the case of the gun fired.*)

A concluding remark to this section: The examples quoted as paradoxes should not be accepted in the logical category of paradoxes that lead to contradictions. The variety of cases is a demonstration for closed world information defects, deficits leading to contradictions in logical reasoning. In a real world project these can be hidden in an abundance of data and cause difficulties in further applications. This list is only a small survey of examples used in the recent and earlier artificial intelligence literature. More demanding lists, well ordered by types of logical mistakes is now available on Wikipedia.

4.1. Skeptics

The following is an extended quote from *Diogenes Laertius* (1895):

> And these ten modes (*tropoi*, singular *tropos*) Phyrrho lays down in the following manner.
>
> The first relates to the difference which one remarks between the sentiments of animals in respect of pleasure, and pain, and what is injurious, and what is advantageous; and from this we conclude, that the same objects do not always produce the same impressions; and that the fact of this difference ought to be a reason with us for suspending our judgment. For there are some animals which are produced without any sexual connection, as those which live in the fire, and the Arabian Phoenix,

and worms. Others again are engendered by copulation, as men and others of that kind; and some are composed in one way, and others in another; on which account they also differ in their senses, as for instance, hawks are very keen-sighted; dogs have a most acute scent. It is plain, therefore, that the things seen produce different impressions on those animals which differ in their power of sight. So, too, young branches are eagerly eaten by the goat, but are bitter to mankind; and hemlock is nutritious for the quail, but deadly to man; and pigs eat their own dung, but a horse does not.

The second mode refers to the nature and idiosyncrasies of men. According to Demophon, the steward of Alexander used to feel warm in the shade, and to shiver in the sun. And Andron, the Argive, as Aristotle tells us, travelled through the dry parts of Libya, without once drinking. Again, one man is fond of medicine, another of farming, another of commerce; and the same pursuits are good for one man, and injurious to another; on which account, we ought to suspend our opinions.

The third mode, is that which has for its object the difference of the organs of sense. Accordingly, an apple presents itself to the sight as yellow, to the taste as sweet, to the smell as fragrant; and the same form is seen, in very different lights, according to the differences of mirrors. It follows, therefore, that what is seen is just as likely to be something else as the reality.

The fourth refers to the dispositions of the subject, and the changes in general to which it is liable. Such as health, sickness, sleep, waking, joy, grief, youth, old age, courage, fear, want, abundance, hatred, friendship, warmth, cold, easiness of breathing, oppression of the respiratory organs, and so on. The objects, therefore, appear different to us according to the disposition of the moment; for, even madmen are not in a state contrary to nature. For, why are we to say that of them more than of ourselves? For we too look at the sun as if it stood still. Theon, of Tithora, the Stoic, used to walk about in his sleep; and a slave of Pericles' used to, when in the same state, walk on the top of the house.

The fifth mode is conversant with laws, and established customs, and belief in mythical traditions, and the conventions of art, and dogmatic opinions. This mode embraces all that relates to vice, and to honesty; to the true, and to the false; to the good, and to the bad; to the Gods, and to the production, and destruction of all visible objects. Accordingly, the same action is just in the case of some people, and unjust in that of others. And good in the case of some, and bad in that of others. On this principle we see that the Persians do not think it unnatural for a man to marry his daughter; but among the Greeks it is unlawful. Again, the Massagetae, as Eudoxus tells us in the first book of his Travels over the World, have their women in common but the Greeks do not. And the Cilicians delight in piracy, but the Greeks avoid it. So again, different nations worship different Gods; and some believe in the providence of God, and others do not. The Egyptians embalm their dead, and then bury them; the Romans burn them; the Paeonians throw them into the lakes. All these considerations show that we ought to suspend our judgment.

The sixth mode has reference to the promiscuousness and confusion of objects; according to which nothing is seen by us simply and by itself; but in combination either with air, or with light, or with moisture, or with solidity, or heat, or cold, or motion, or evaporation or some other power. Accordingly, purple exhibits a different hue in the sun, and in the moon, and in a lamp. And our own complexions appear different when seen at noonday and at sunset. And a stone which one cannot lift in the air, is easily displaced in the water, either because it is heavy itself and is made light by the water, or because it is light in itself and is made heavy by the air. So that we cannot positively know the peculiar qualities of anything, just as we cannot discover oil in ointment.

The seventh mode has reference to distances, and position, and space, and to the objects which are in space. In this mode one establishes the fact that objects which we believe to be large, sometimes appear small; that those which we believe to be square, sometimes appear round; that those which we fancy even, appear full of projections; those which we think straight, seem bent; and those which we believe to be colorless, appear of quite a different complexion. Accordingly, the sun, on account of its distance from us, appears small. The mountains too, at a distance, appear airy masses and smooth, but when beheld close, they are rough. Again, the sun has one appearance at his rise, and quite a different one at midday. And the same body looks very different in a wood from what it does on plain ground. So too, the appearance of an object changes according to its position as regards us; for instance, the neck of a dove varies as it turns. Since then, it is impossible to view these things irrespectively of place and position, it is clear that their real nature is not known.

The eighth mode has respect to the magnitudes or quantities of things; or to the heat or coldness, or to the speed or slowness, or to the paleness or variety of color of the subject. For instance, a moderate quantity of wine when taken invigorates, but an excessive quantity weakens. And the same is the case with food, and other similar things.

The ninth depends upon the frequency, or rarity, or strangeness of the thing under consideration. For instance, earthquakes excite no wonder among those nations with whom they are of frequent occurrence nor does the sun, because he is seen every day.

The ninth mode is called by *Phavorinus,* the eighth, and by *Sextus* and *Aenesidemus,* the tenth; and *Sextus* calls the tenth the eighth, which *Phavorinus* reckons the tenth as the ninth in order.

The tenth mode refers to the comparison between one thing and another; as, for instance, between what is light and what is heavy; between what is strong and what is weak; between what is greater and what is less; what is above and what is below. For instance, that which is on the right, is not on the right intrinsically and by nature, but it is looked upon as such in consequence of its relation to something else; and if that other thing be transposed, then it will no longer be on the right. In the same way, a man is spoken of as a father, or brother, or relation to some one else; and day is called so in relation to the sun: and everything has its distinctive name in relation to human thought: therefore, those things which are known in relation to others, are unknown of themselves.

And these are the ten modes.

4.2. Voting, Games

Ordering preferences is one of deepest epistemic problems of all societies. This is an old problem, and voting for positions in a community is only one application aspect of voting systems. It received a mathematically correct treatment *in impossibility theory* by the work of Kenneth J. Arrow, in 1951 (*Social Choice and Individual Values*, New Haven, Yale UP). Arrow proved this impossibility for three or more individual, independent choices. The problem having a long past, the first documented deliberation, with a rather clear notational demonstration, is due to the ingenious Raymond(us) Lull(us), from the 13th c. Lullus was also the designer of a logical proof machine for the existence of God. The election studies were recommendations for election of prelates and abbesses.

The controversies on the basic voting schemes, of the (simple) majority vote and of pair-wise comparisons, returned at the advent of

Endgame

modern democratic societies, first with Jean-Charles de Borda and the Marquis de Condorcet, just before the French Revolution.

From an epistemic point of view, the *impossibility theorem* can be similar to the Gödelian *incompleteness* and *undecidability* theorems, though they had very different motivations, and different ways of mathematical reasoning. The problem is a cardinal question in weighting points of views, preferences, and classifications for selection. Modern game theories try to approach the problem with probabilistic-statistical and psychological-social methods.

References

Aaronson, S. (2008). The Limits of Quantum. Scientific American, March: 50-57.

Aczél, J., Falmagne, J. C. and Luce, R.D. (2000). Functional Equations in the Behavioral Sciences. Math. Japonica, 52, 469-512.

Akerlof, G. A. (1970). The Market for 'Lemons': Quality Uncertainty and the Market Mechanism. Quarterly Journal of Economics 84, no. 3, 488-500.

Akerlof, G. A., Shiller, R. J. (2009). Animal Spirits: How Human Psychology Drives The Economy, And Why It Matters for Global Capitalism. Princeton: Princeton University Press.

Andréka, H., Madarász, J. X. and Németi, I. (2006). Logical Axiomatizations of Space-time in Non-Euclidean Geometries: János Bolyai Memorial Volume, eds. Prékopa, A. and E. Molnár. Berlin: Springer, 155-85.

Aristotle. (1984). Metaphysics, trans. William David Ross, vol. 2 of Complete Works: the Revised Oxford Translation, ed. Barnes, J., 2 Vols. Princeton: Princeton University Press, 1552-1728.

Arrow, K. J. (1951). Social Choice and Individual Values. New Haven: Yale University Press.

Aumann, R. J. (1974). Subjectivity and Correlation in Randomized Strategies. Journal of Mathematical Economics 1, 67-96.

Aumann, R. J. (1987). Game Theory in: The New Palgrave Dictionary of Economics, eds. Eatwell, J., Milgate, M. and P. Newman. London: Macmillan, 460-82.

Babbage, C. (1961) in: Charles Babbage and his Calculating Engines—Selected Writings by Charles Babbage and Others, eds. Moseley, M., Morrison, P. and E. Morrison. New York: Dover Publications.

Backus, J. (1959). The Syntax and Semantics of the Proposed International Algebraic Language of the Zurich ACM-GAMM Conference—The First World Computer Congress. Paris: IFIP/UNESCO, 125-31.

Ball, P. (2008). Triumph of the Medieval Mind. Nature 452, April 17, 816-18.

Barabási, A. L. (2002). Linked: The New Science of Networks, Cambridge, Mass.: Perseus Publishing.

Barcan Marcus, R. (1961). Modalities and Intensional Languages. Synthese 13, no. 4, 303–22.

Bayes, T. (1964). Essay Towards Solving a Problem in the Doctrine of Chances. (Published posthumously by his friend Richard Price.) Philosophical Transactions of the Royal Society of London 53 (1764), 370–418.

Bell, A. F. G. (1925). Francisco Sanchez, el Brocense. Oxford: Oxford University Press.

Bernoulli, J. (1713). Ars conjectandi, opus posthumum. Accedit tractatus de seriebus infinitis, et epistola gallicè scripta de ludo pilae reticularis. Basel: Thurneisen Brothers.

Bernoulli, J. (2005). The Art of Conjecturing, together with Letter to a Friend on Sets in Court Tennis. trans. Edith Sylla. Baltimore: John Hopkins University Press. (Original work published 1713).

Bertsekas, D. P. and Tsitsiklis, J. N. (2008). Introduction to Probability, 2nd ed. Cambridge, Mass.: MIT Press.

Black, M. (1937). Vagueness–An Exercise in Logical Analysis. Philosophy of Science 4. 427–55.

Black, F. and Scholes, M. (1973). The Pricing of Options and Corporate Liabilities. Journal of Political Economy 81, no. 3, 637–654.

Bloor, D. (1976). Knowledge and Social Imaginary. London: Routledge and Kegan Paul.

Blum, L., Cucker, F., Shub, M., Smale, S. (1998). Complexity and Real Computation. Berlin: Springer.

Bollobás, B., Varopoulos, N. T. (1975). Representation of Systems of Measurable Sets. Math. Proc. Cambridge Philos. Soc. 78, no. 2, 323–325.

Bolyai, J. "Appendix" in Bolyai F. (1832) Tentamen iuventum studiosam in elementa matheoseos purae, elementaris ac sublimiotis, methodo intuitive, evidentiaque huic propria, introducendi. Maros Vásárhelyini: Collegium Reformatorum.

Boole, G. (1854) An Investigation of the Laws of Thought, accessible by the Gutenberg Project, e-text 15114.

Bolzano, B. (1817). Rein analytischer Beweis des Lehrsatzes, daß zwischen zwei Werten , die ein entgegensetztes Resultat gewähren, wenigstens eine reelle Wurzel der Gleichung liege, Prag, Purely Analytic Proof of The Theorem That between Any Two Values, Which Give Results of Opposite Sign, There Lies at Least One real Root of The Equation in English translation of Bolzano's mathematical writings, Russ S. 225–248, 251–277. (2004)

Borel, E. (1921). La Théorie du Jeu et les Équations Intégrales à Noyau Symétrique. Comptes Rendus de l'Academie des Sciences 173, 1304–1308. "The theory of play and integral equations with skew symmetric kernels", transl. L. J. Savage, Econometrica 21 (1953): 97–100.

Borda, J. C. de (1770). "Mémoire sur les élections au scrutiny" in the Histoire de l'Académie Royale des Sciences, Paris, 1781.

Bourbaki, N. (collective pseudonym, see e.g. Cartan, Dieudonné, Weil) (1958–98) Éléments de Mathémathique. Paris: Masson-Dunod, in English: New York: Springer, 1987–1994.

Bowles, S. (2008). Policies Designed for Self-Interested Citizens May Undermine "The Moral Sentiments": Evidence from Economic Experiments. Science 320, 1605–1609.

Bridges, J. H. ed. (1900). The "Opus Majus" of Roger Bacon. London: Williams and Norgate, (Latin).

Brouwer, L. E. J. (1975). Collected Works 1. Philosophy and Foundations of Mathematics, ed. Heyting, A. Amsterdam: North-Holland.

Buchanan, J. M., Tullock, G. (1962). The Calculus of Consent, Logical Foundations of Constitutional Democracy. Ann Arbor: The University of Michigan Press.

Butler, S. (1663). Hudibras. London. Facsimile ed. New York: Scholars' Facsimiles & Reprints, 1994.

Cantor, G. (1915) Contributions to the Founding of the Theory of Transfinite Numbers. New York: Dover Publications, 1955.

Čapek, Karel (1920) R.U.R. (Rossum's Universal Robots), English trans. David Wyllie, eBooks@Adelaide, 2006.

Cayley, A. (1889–1897). The collected mathematical papers of Arthur Cayley. Cambridge: Cambridge University Press.

Ceruzzi, P. E. (1998). A History of Modern Computing. Cambridge, Mass.: MIT Press.

Chaitin, G. J. (1987). Information, Randomness and Incompleteness–Papers on Algorithmic Information Theory. Singapore: World Scientific.

Chaitin, G. (2006). The Limits of Reason. Scientific American (March): 54–61.

Chomsky, N. (1957). Syntactic Structures. The Hague: Mouton.

Church, A. (1936). An unsolvable problem of elementary number theory. American Journal of Mathematics 58, 345–363.

Church, A. (1941). Introduction to Mathematical Logic. Princeton, NJ: Princeton University Press.

Church, A. (1956). The Calculi of Lambda Conversion. Princeton, NJ: Princeton University Press.

Cochrane, C.N. (1944). Christianity and Classical Culture: A Study of Thought and Action from Augustus to Augustine. London: Oxford University Press.

Colebrooke, H. T. (1817). Algebra, with Arithmetic and Mensuration from the Sanscrit of Brahmagupta and Bhaskara. London: J. Murray.

Condorcet, M. J. A. N. (1785). Essay on the Application of [mathematical] Analysis to the Probability of Majority Decisions.

Condorcet, M. J. A. N. (1947–49). Oeuvres, 12 vols, eds. Condorcet O'Connor, A. and M.F. Arago, 1847–1849.

Crombie, A. C. (1995). Styles of Scientific Thinking in the European Tradition: The History of Argument and Explanation Especially in the Mathematical and Biomedical Sciences and Arts. London: Gerald Duckworth & Company.

Craw, S., Wiratunge, N., Rowe, R. C. (2006). Learning Adaptation Knowledge to Improve Case-Based Reasoning." Artificial Intelligence 170, 1175–1192.

Dantzig, G. (1953) Notes on Linear Programming. Santa Monica, Calif.: Rand Corporation.

Darwin, Charles. (1859). The Origin of Species by Means of Natural Selection. London: John Murray, 1872; New York: Random House Value Publishing, 1979.

Davis, M., ed. (1965). The Undecidable, Basic Papers on Undecidable Propositions, Unsolvable Problems and Computable Functions. Raven Press, Hewitt, New York, Updated and new versions in Dover, Mineola, New York, 2004.

Dehaene, S., Izard, V., Spelke, E., Pica, P. (2008). Log or Linear? Distinct Intuitions of the Number Scale in Western and Amazonian Indigene Cultures. Science 320 (May 30), 1217–1223.

Diermeier, D. (2007). Arguing for Computational Power. Science 318 (November 9), 918–919.

de Kleer, J. (1986). "Qualitative Physics" in Encyclopedia of Artificial Intelligence, ed. Shapiro Stuart C. New York: John Wiley.

de Morgan, A. (1849). Trigonometry and Double Algebra. London: Talyor, Walton & Malbery.

de Morgan, A. (1872). A Budget of Paradoxes. New York: Dover Publications.

Dedekind, R. R. J. (1932). Gesammelte mathematische Werke. Braunschweig: Vieweg, Reprint: New York, 1969.

Dedekind, R. R. J. (2005). Essays on the Theory of Numbers. In God Created the Integers, ed. Hawking, S. Philadephia: Running Press, 906–964.

Dempster, A. P. (2008). The Dempster-Shafer Calculus for Statisticians. Int.J. Approx. Reasoning, 48, no. 2, 365–377.

Dennett, D. C. (1995). Darwin's Dangerous Idea. New York: Simon & Schuster.

Descartes, R. (1887–1913). Oeuvres de Descartes, eds. Adam, C. and P. Tannery. Paris: Vrin.

Descartes, R. (1984–1991). The philosophical Writings of Descartes, trans. John Cottingham, Robert Stoothoff, Dugald Murdoch and Anthony Kenny. Cambridge: Cambridge University Press, 3 vols.

Dieudonné, J. A. E. (1987). Pour l'honneur de l'esprit humain. Les mathématiques aujourd'hi. Paris: Hachette Pluriel, 10.

Diogenes, L. (1862). De Clarorum Philosophorum Vitis, Dogmatibus et Apophtegmatibus, Paris: Didot.Trans. R. D. Hicks, Lives of Eminent Philosophers. Cambridge, Mass.: Harvard University Press, Loeb Classical Library, 1925.

Diophantos of Alexandria (1885). in T. L. Heath, Diophantos of Alexandria: A Study in the History of Greek Algebra. Cambridge: Cambridge University Press, 1885, 1910.

Diophantos of Alexandria (2005). A Study in the History of Greek Algebra. In: God Created the Integers, ed. Hawking, S. Philadelphia: Running Press, 244-284.

Dirac, P. (1983). Hidden Geometry—Interview with Thomas Kuhn. Nature 437 (September 15), 32.

Doyle, J. (1979). A truth maintenance system. Artificial Intelligence 12, 231-272.

Doyle, J. (1983). What Is Rational Psychology? AI Magazine 4, 50-54.

Dreyfus, H. (1992). What Computers Still Can't Do: A Critique of Artificial Reason. Cambridge, Mass.: MIT Press.

Eiter, T., Ianni, G., Lukasiewicz, T., Schindlauer, R., Tompits, H. (2008). Combining Answer Set Programming with Description Logics for the Semantic Web. Artificial Intelligence 172, 1495-1439.

Euclide. (1956). Elements, trans. Thomas Heath. Mineola, N.Y.: Dover Publications.

Érdi, P. (2008). Complexity Explained, New York: Springer.

Foote, R. (2007). Mathematics and Complex Systems. Science 318 (October 19), 410-12.

Fourier, J. B. J. (1882). Théorie analytique de la chaleur. Paris: F. Dido.

Fourier, J. B. J. (2003). The Analytical Theory of Heat, trans. Alexander Freeman. Mineola, N.Y.: Dover.

Fraenkel, A., Bar-Hillel, Y., Levy, A. (1958). Foundations of Set Theory. Amsterdam: North Holland.

Frege, G. (1879). Begriffsschrift, eine der arithmetischen nachgebildeten Formelsprachen des reines Denkens. Halle: Nebert.

Frege, G. (1967). Concept Script, A Formal Language of Pur Tthought Modelled upon That of Arithmetic, trans. Stefan Bauer-Mengelberg in From Frege to Gödel: A Source Book in Mathematical Logic, 1879-1931, ed. van Heijenoort, J., Cambridge, Mass.: Harvard University Press.

Galois, É. (1846). OEuvres mathématiques d'Évariste Galois. Journal des mathématiques pures et appliquées XI, 381-444.

Gardner, M. (1970). Mathematical Games: The fantastic Combinations of John Conway's New Solitaire Game "Life". Scientific American 223 (October), 120-123.

Gassendi, P. (1964). Opera Omnia. 6 Vols. Reproduction of 1658 Edition with introduction by Tullio Gregory, Stuttgart-Bad Cannstatt: Friedrich Frommann Verlag. Selected Works, trans. Craig Brush (Texts in Early Modern Philosophy). New York: Johnson Reprint, 1972.

Ginsberg, M. L. (1986). Counterfactuals, Artificial Intelligence, 30: 35-79.

Gosset, W. S. (Student) (1904). The Application of the "Law of Error" to the Work of the Brewery—nota interna presso. Guinnes. "The Probable Error of a Mean." Biometrika 6, no. 1 (March 1908): 1-25.

Gödel, K. (1931). Über formal unentscheidbare Sätze der Principia Mathematica und verwandter Systeme. Monatshefte für Mathematik und Physik 38, 173-198.

Gödel, K. (1930). The completeness of the axioms of the functional calculus of logic in van Heijenoort, J. From Frege to Gödel—A Source Book in Mathematical Logic, 1879-1931. Cambridge, Mass.: Harvard University Press, 1967, 582-591.

Gödel, K. (1931). "On formally undecidable propositions of Principia Mathematica and related systems" in van Heijenoort, J. From Frege to Gödel—A Source Book in Mathematical Logic, 1879-1931. Cambridge, Mass.: Harvard University Press, 1967, 596-616.

Goethe, J. W. (1982). Goethes Werke, Hamburger Ausgabe in 14 Bänden, textkritisch durchgesehen und kommentiert von Erich Trunz, 13. Aufl. München: C. H. Beck. Works by Johann Wolfgang von Goethe at Project Gutenberg.

Goldstine, H. H. (1972). The Computer from Pascal to von Neumann. New Jersey: Princeton University Press.

González, M. C., Hidalgo, C. A., Barabási, A. L. (2008). Understanding Individual Human Mobility Patterns. Nature 453 (June 5), 779-782.

Greene, M. (2004). The birth of modern science?—Review on L. Russo (transl. Silvio Levy): The forgotten revolution: How science was born in 300 BC and why it had to be reborn. Nature 430 (August 5), 614.

Gromov, M. (1999). Metric Structures for Riemannian and Non-Riemannian Spaces. Boston: Birkhauser.

Grosseteste, R. (1912). Die Philosophischen Werke des Robert Grosseteste, Bischofs von Lincoln. Ed. Baur, L. Beiträge zur Geschichte der Philosophie des Mittelalters, 9. Münster: Aschendorff Verlag, 1912. http://www.grosseteste.com/: the Electronic Grosseteste.

Hacking, I. (1975). The Emergence of Probability—A Philosophical Study of Early Ideas about Probability, Induction And Statistical Inference. Cambridge: Cambridge University Press.

Haenni, R. and S. Hartmann. (2006). Special Issue of Minds and Machines on Causality, Uncertainty and Ignorance. Minds and Machines 16, no. 3, 237–238.

Halpern, J. Y. (2005) Reasoning About Uncertainty, Cambridge, Mass.: MIT Press, 2003, slightly revised 2005.

Halpern, J. Y.; Y. Moses. (2007) Characterizing Solution Concepts in Games Using Knowledge-Based Programs. Proceedings of the 20th International Joint Conference on Artificial Intelligence (IJCAI 2007), 1300–1307.

Halpern, J.; Pearl, J. (2001) Causes and explanations: A structural-model approach in Proc. of the Seventeenth Conference on Uncertainty in Artificial Intelligence. San Francisco, CA: Morgan Kaufmann, 194–202.

Hamilton, W. R. (1853). Lectures on Quaternions. Dublin: Royal Irish Academy.

Hamilton, W. R. (1931-1967). The Mathematical Papers. Cambridge: Cambridge University Press.

Hanks, S. and McDermott, D., 1987. Nonmonotonic logic and temporal projection. Artificial Intelligence, 33:279-412

Harel, D. (1992). Algorithmics. The Spirit of Computing. New York: Addison-Wesley.

Harsányi, J. C. (1967-68) Games with Incomplete Information Played by 'Bayesian' Players." Management Science 14, 159-182, 320–334, 486–502.

Hawking, S. W. (2005). God Created the Integers. Philadelphia: Running Press, 2005.

van Heijenoort, J., ed. (1967). From Frege to Gödel—seminal papers between 1879 and 1931. Cambridge, Mass.: Harvard University Press.

Hilbert, D. (1900). Mathematische Probleme-Vortrag, gehalten auf dem internationalen Mathematiker-Kongress zu Paris 1900, in Nachrichten von der Königlichen Gesellschaft der Wissenschaften zu Göttingen, 253–297. "Mathematical Problems"—lecture delivered before the International Congress of Mathematicians at Paris 1900, trans. Dr. Maby Winton Newson with the author's permission for Bulletin of the American Mathematical Society 8 (1902): 437–479.

Hilbert, D. (1928). Die Grundlagen der Mathematik. Mit Zusätzen von Hermann Weyl und Paul Bernays, Hamburger Mathematische Einzelschriften 5 (1928): 1–21, Leipzig: Teubner, Works by David Hilbert at Project Gutenberg

Hofstadter, D. R. (1979). Gödel, Escher, Bach: An Eternal Golden Braid. New York: Basic Books.

Hromkovic, J. (2002). Algorithmics for Hard Problems. New York: Springer.

Hume, D. A. (1739–40). Treatise of Human Nature—Being an Attempt to Introduce The Experimental Method of Reasoning into Moral Subjects, ed. Selby-Bigge, L. A., 2nd ed. revised by Nidditch, P.H. Oxford: Clarendon Press, 1975.

Huizinga, J. (1937). The Waning of the Middle Ages, London: Edward Arnold & Co.Hurwicz, L. and S. Reiter. (2006) Designing Economic Mechanisms. Cambridge: Cambridge University Press.

Hurwicz, L. (1972). On Informationally Decentralized Systems in Decision and Organization, eds. Radner, R. and B. McGuire. Amsterdam: North-Holland, 2008, 297–336.

Hurwitz, L. (2008). But Who Will Guard the Guardians? American Economic Review 98, no. 3 (June): 577–585.

Jaeger, G. (2007). Quantum Information—An Overview. New York: Springer.

Khachian, L. H. (1979) A polynomial algorithm in linear programming (in Russian) Doklady Akad. Nauk SSSR 244, no. 5, 1093–1096.

Kahneman, D.; A. Tversky. (1972). Subjective Probability: A Judgement of Representativeness. Cognitive Psychology 3, 430–454.

Kandel E. R., Schwartz J.H., Jessell T.M. (2000). Principles of Neural Science, 4th ed. McGraw-Hill, New York.

Kandel, E. R., and L. Tauc L. (1965). Mechanism of heterosynaptic facilitation in the giant cell of the abdominal ganglion of Aplysia depilans. J. Physiol. (London). 181:28.

Kapoor, K. (2005) Dimensions of Panini Grammar: The Indian Grammatical System. New Delhi: D.K. Printworld.

Karinthy, F.: Minden másképpen van (in Hungarian) (Everything is different)–Ötvenkét vasárnap (Fifty two Sundays), Láncszemek (Chain-Links), Budapest: Athenaeum 1929. Trans. and annot. Adam Makkai, 2nd rev. ed. 2000. in: Newman, M., Barabási, A.-L., Watts, D.J.: The Structure of Dynamics of Networks, Prenceton: Princeton University Press, 2006, 21–26.

Karmarkar, N. (1984). A New Polynomial Time Algorithm for Linear Programming." Combinatorica 4, 373–395.

Kauffman, S. A. (1993). The Origins of Order, Self -Organization and Selection in Evolution. New York: Oxford University Press.

Kemp, M. (2004). Platonic Puppetry—on Attila Csörgö's Kinetic Sculptures. Nature 428 (April 22), 803.

Kempf, G. R. (1993). Algebraic Variations. London Mathematical Society Lecture Note Series 172. Cambridge: Cambridge University Press.

Kneale, W. and M. Kneale. (1971) The Development of Logic. Oxford: Oxford University Press.

Kolmogoroff, A. N. (1933) Grundbegriffe der Wahrscheinlichkeitsrechnung. Berlin–Heidelberg: Springer.

Kolmogorov, A. N. (1965) Three Approaches to the Concept of 'the Amount of Information'." Problems of Information Transmission 1, 1–7.

Kolmogorov, A. N. (1968). Logical Basis for information theory and probability theory. IEEE Trans. on Information Theory IT-14, 662–664.

Kolmogorov A.N. (1925) On the Principle of Excluded Middle. (in Russian) Matematicheskiy Sbornik 646–667. English in From Frege to Gödel–A Source Book in Mathematical Logic, 1879–1931, ed. van Heijenhoort, J. Cambridge, Mass.: Harvard University Press, 1967, 414–437.

Kornai, A. (2007). Mathematical Linguistics. Berlin–Heidelberg: Springer.

Kripke, S. A. (1971). Semantical Considerations on Modal Logic. In Reference and Modality, ed. Linsky, L. London: Oxford University Press, 63–72.

Kripke, S. A. (1972). Naming and necessity. In Semantics of Natural Languages, eds. Harmon, G. and D. Davidson. Dordrecht: Reidel, 253–355.

Kuhn, T. S. (1962) The Structure of Scientific Revolutions. Chicago, Ill.: University of Chicago Press.

Lagrange, J. L. (1888-1889) Mécanique Analytique, 4. ed., 2 vols. Paris: Gauthier-Villars et fils.

Lakatos, I. (1963-64). Proofs and Refutations. British Journal of Philosophical Science 14, 1–25, 120–39, 221–43, 296–342.

Lakatos, I. (1970). Falsification and the methodology of scientific research programmes, in Criticism and the Growth of Knowledge, ed. Lakatos, I. and A. Musgrave. Cambridge: Cambridge University Press, 91–196.

Lakoff, G., Johnson, M. (1999). Philosophy In the Flesh: The Embodied Mind and Its Challenge to Western Thought. New York: Basic Books.

Laplace, P. S. (1878-1912). Œuvres complètes de Laplace, 14 vols. Paris: Gauthier-Villars, 1878-1912.

Lazos, Christos. (1998). Engineering and Technology in Ancient Greece, Trans.: Margie Lazou, Laboratory for Automation and Robotics, University of Patras, Athens

Leibniz, G. W. (1768). Opera Omnia. Ed. Dutens, L. Geneva.

Leibniz, G. W. (1898). The Monadology and Other Philosophical Writings. Oxford: Oxford University Press.

Leibniz, G. W. (1960). Fragmente zur Logic. Berlin: Akademie Verlag, 1960.

Lenstra, A. K., Lenstra; H. W., Jr., Lovász, L. (1982). Factoring Polynomials with Integer Coefficients." Mathematische Annalen 261, 513–534.

Lenstra, H. (2003). Escher And The Droste Effect. Leiden: Universiteit Leiden, http://escherdroste.math.leidenuniv.nl/.

Leontief, W. W. (1986). Input-Output Economics. 2nd ed. New York: Oxford University Press, 1986.

Lie, S. M. (1888-93) Theorie der Transformationsgruppen, 3 vols. (Theory of Transformation Groups). Leipzig: Teubner.

Lobachevsky, N. I. (1837). Géométrie imaginaire. Journal für die reine und angewandte Mathematik 17, 295–320.

Lobachevsky, N. I. (1840). Geometrische Untersuchungen zur Theorie der Parallellinien. Berlin: F. Fincke. English trans. in: G. B. Halsted printed as a supplement to Bonola, R., Non-Euclidean Geometry: A critical and historical study of its development, 1955; English trans.with additional appendices by H.S. Carslaw. New York: 1955.

Löwenheim, L. (1915). Über Möglichkeiten im Relativkalkül." Math. Ann. 68, 169–207. (On possibilities in the calculus of relatives–trans. in From Frege to Gödel–A Source Book in Mathematical Logic, 1879-1931. ed. van Heijenoort, J. Cambridge, Mass.: Harvard University Press, 1971.

Mackenzie, D. (2005). What in The Name of Euclid Is Going on Here? Science 307 (March 4), 1402–1403.

Muggleton, S., Otero, R., Colton, S. (2008). Guest Editorial: Special Issue on Inductive Logic Programming. Machine Learning 70, no. 2–3, 119–120.

Mandelbrot, B. (1977). Fractals: Form, Chance and Dimension. New York: W. H. Freeman & Co.

Mandelbrot, B. (1982). The Fractal Geometry of Nature. New York: W. H. Freeman & Co.

Marchiori, D.; Warglien, M. (2008). Predicting Human Interactive Learning by Regret-Driven Neural Networks. Science 319 (February 22), 1111–1113.

Marenbon, J. (1997). The Philosophy of Peter Abelard. Cambridge: Cambridge University Press.

Markov, A. A. (1906). Распространение закона больших чисел на величины, зависящие друг от друга (Rasprostranenie zakona bol'shih chisel na velichiny, zavisyaschie drug ot druga). Известия Физико-математического общества при Казанском университете (Izvestiya fiziko-matematicheskogo obschestva pri Kazanskom universitete) 2, no. 15, 135–156.

Markov, A.A. (1971). Extension of The Limit Theorems of Probability Theory to A Sum of Variables Connected in A Chain. Reprinted in Appendix B of Howard, R. Dynamic Probabilistic Systems, volume 1: Markov Chains. New York: John Wiley and Sons.

Maskin, E. S., Simonovits, A. (2000). Planning, Shortage and Transformation. Cambridge, Mass.: MIT Press.

Maskin, E. S. ed. (1999). Recent Developments in Game Theory. London: Edward Elgar Publ.

Mazur, B. (2006). Controlling Our Errors. Nature 443 (September 7), 38–39.

Maxwell, J. C. "On Governors." Proceedings of the Royal Society 16 (1867–1868): 270–283.

Maxwell, J. C. (1873). A Treatise on Electricity And Magnetism. Oxford: Clarendon Press.

McCarthy, J. (1968). Programs with Common Sense in Semantic Information Processing, ed. Minsky, M. L. Cambridge, Mass.: MIT Press.

McCarthy, J.P., Hayes, J. (1969). Some Philosophical Problems from the Standpoint of Artificial Intelligence in Machine Intelligence, ed. Meltzer, B. and D. Michie, vol. 4. Edinburgh: Edinburgh University Press, 463–502.

McCarthy, J. (1977). Epistemological Problems of Artificial Intelligence. Proc. IJCAI'77. Cambridge, Mass.: MIT Press, 1038-1044.

McCarthy, J. (1980). Circumscription: A form of Non-Monotonic Reasoning. Artificial Intelligence 13, 27-40.

McCarthy, J. (1986). Applications of Circumscription to Formalizing Common-Sense Knowledge. Artificial Intelligence 28 (1986), 89-116.

Minsky, L. M. (1985). The Society of Mind. New York: Simon & Schuster.

Minsky, L. M. (2006). The Emotion Machine. New York: Simon & Schuster.

Monostori, L., Váncza, J. and Kumara, S.R.T. (2006). Agent-Based Systems for Manufacturing–keynote paper. CIRP Annals–Manufacturing Technology 55, no. 2 , 697-720.

Moore, R.C. (1985). Semantic considerations on nonmonotonic logic. Artificial Intelligence, 25 (no. 1): 75-94

Myerson, R. B. (1991). Game Theory: Analysis of Conflict. Cambridge, Mass.: Harvard University Press.

Nash, J. F. Jr. (1950). Equilibrium Points in N-Person Games. Proceedings of the National Academy of Sciences 36, 48-49.

Nash, J. F. Jr. (1950). The Bargaining Problem. Econometrica 18, 155-162.

Nash, J. F. Jr. (1951). Non-Cooperative Games. Annals of Mathematics 54, 286-295.

Nash, J. F. Jr. (1953). Two-Person Cooperative Game. Econometrica 21, 128-140.

Naur, P. (1992). Computing: A Human Activity–Selected Writings from 1951 to 1990. New York: ACM Press/Addison-Wesley.

Neumann, J. v. (1928) Zur Theorie der Gesellschaftsspiele. Math. Ann. 100, 295-320. Trans. S. Bargmann: On the Theory of Games of Strategy in Contributions to the Theory of Games, Vol. IV (Ann. Math. Studies, no. 40). Princeton: Princeton University Press, 1959, 13-42.

Neumann, J. v.; D. Morgenstern. (1944). Theory of Games and Economic Behaviour. Princeton: Princeton University Press. (Subsequent, enlarged editions: 1947, 1953.)

Neumann, J. v. (1949). Recent theories of turbulence in Collected Works, ed. Taub, A. H. Oxford: Pergamon Press, 1963.

Neumann, J. v. (1958). The Computer and the Brain–Silliman Lectures. New Haven: Yale University Press.

Neumann, J. v. (1955). Can We Survive Technology? Fortune (June): 151-52.

Neumann, J. v. (1956). Probabilistic Logics And The Synthesis of Reliable Organisms from Unreliable components" (January 1952) Calif. Inst. of Techn., Lecture notes taken by R. S. Pierce and revised by the author, in Automata Studies, eds. Shannon, C. E. and J. McCarthy. Princeton: Princeton University Press, 43-98.

Neumann, J. v. "The Impact of Recent Developments in Science on the Economy And on Economics." Partial text of a talk at the National Planning Assoc., Washington, D. C., December 12, 1955, Looking Ahead 4, (1956): 11

Neumann, J. v. (1937, ca.). Quantum Logics (Strict- and Probability-Logics)–manuscript, unfinished, reviewed by A. H. Taub, in Collected Works, IV: 195-97.

Neumann, J. v. (1966). Theory of Self-Reproducing Automata, ed. and completed by Burks, A. W. Urbana: University of Illinois Press.

Neumann, J. v., Goldstine, H. H. (1990). On the Principles of Large Scale Computing Machines–manuscript (1946), in The Legacy of John von Neumann eds. Glimm, J., Impagliazzo, J. and I. Singer. Providence, R.I.: Amer. Math. Soc.

Newman, M., Barabási, A., Watts, D.J. (2009). The Structure and Dynamics of Networks. Princeton: Princeton University Press.

Newton, I. (1978). Papers and Letters in Natural Philosophy, ed. Cohen, I. B. Cambridge, Mass.: Harvard University Press.

Newton, I. (1999). The Principia, A New Translation. Guide by Cohen, I. B. Berkeley: University of California Press.

Nicolai, H. (2007). A Beauty and a Beast. Nature 447 (May 3,), 41-42.

Nietzsche, F. (1993). Also sprach Zarathustra, ed. Colli, G. and M. Montinari, (study edition of the standard German Nietzsche edition) Munich: Deutscher Taschenbuch Verlag. In English: Thus Spoke Zarathustra, trans. Walter Kaufmann. New York: Random House, 1995.

Noether, E. A. (1983). Gesammelte Abhandlungen (Collected Works), ed. Jacobson, N. Berlin, New York: Springer-Verlag.

Norman, D. (2004). Why Machines Should Fear?–interview with Wayt W. Gibbs. Scientific American (January), 27.

O'Shea, D. (2007). What Do Mathematicians Do?–Review on W. Byers: How Mathematicians Think: Using Ambiguity, Contradiction, and Paradox to Create Mathematics. Princeton University Press, 2007; D. Ruelle: The Mathematician's Brain: A Personal Tour Through the Essentials of Mathematics and Some of the Great Minds Behind Them, Princeton Univ. Press, 2007; and on M. Fitzgerald and I. James: The Mind of the Mathematician, Johns Hopkins Univ. Press, Nature 449 (October 25) 982-83.

Pagel, M. (2008). Rise of the Digital Machine. Nature 452 (April 10), 699.

Pareto, V. (1906). Manuale d'economia politica. Milan: Società Editrice Libraria. In English: Manual of Political Economy trans. Vilfredo Pareto and Ann S. Schwier, ed. Page A. N. and Ann S. Schwier. New York: A. M. Kelley, 1971.

Parsons, T. and Smelser, N. J. (1956). Economy and Society: International Library of Sociology B: Economics and Society–reprint, London: Routledge, 2003

Pascal, B. (1904). Pensées et Opuscules, publiés par M. Brunschvicg, Paris: Hachette.

Pascal, B. (1960). Oeuvres complètes. Paris: Seuil.

Pascal, B. (1909-14). Thoughts. Trans. W. F. Trotter, ed. Charles W. Eliot, Harvard Classics, Vol. 48, Part 1, New York: P.F. Collier & Son.

Peano, G. (1889). The Principles of Arithmetic, Presented by a New Method, In: From Frege to Gödel–A Source Book in Mathematical Logic, 1879–1931, ed. van Heijenoort, J. Cambridge, Mass.: Harvard University Press, 1967), 83-97.

Pearl, J. (1988). Probabilistic Reasoning in Intelligent Systems, San Mateo, CA: Morgan Kaufmann.

Pearl, J. (2000). Causality: Models, Reasoning, and Inference. Cambridge: Cambridge University Press.

Pearl, J. (2004). Robustness in Causal Claims in Proc. of the 20th Conference on Uncertainty in Artificial Intelligence. Arlington, Virginia: AUAI Press, 446-453.

Pena, A., Sossa, H., Gutiérrez, A. (2008). Causal Knowledge and Reasoning by Cognitive Maps: Pursuing a Holistic Approach." Expert Systems with Applications 35, 2-18.

Penrose, R. (1989). The Emperor's New Mind. Oxford: Oxford University Press.

Penrose, R. (1994). Shadows of the Mind–A Search for the Missing Science of Consciousness. New York: Oxford University Press.

Penrose, R. (2004). The Road to Reality, A Complete Guide to the Laws of the Universe. Random House, N.Y.: Vintage Books.

Plato. (1997). Complete Works, ed. Cooper, J. M. and D. S. Hutchinson (Associate Editor). Indianapolis: Hackett Publishing Company.

Poisson, S. D. (1809). Sur la variation des constantes arbitraires dans les questions de Mécanique. J. de l'École Polytech. 8, 266-353.

Popper, K. (1963). Conjectures and Refutations: The Growth of Scientific Knowledge. London: Routledge and Kegan Paul.

Post, E. L. (1943). Formal Reductions of the General Combinatorial Decision Problem. American Journal of Mathematics 65, 197-215.

Post, E. L. (1944). Recursively enumerable sets of positive integers and their decision problems. Bulletin of the American Mathematical Society 50, 284-316.

Price, D. J. de Solla (1961). Science since Babylon. New Haven: Yale University Press.

Ramsay, F. P. (1931). The Foundations of Mathematics and Other Logical Essays. London: Kegan Paul.

Richard, J. (1905). Les principes des mathématiques et le problème des ensembles." Revue générale des sciences pures et appliquées 16, 541–543. In English: The principles of mathematics and the problem of sets, in van Heijenoort, J. From Frege to Gödel–A Source Book in Mathematical Logic, 1879–1931. Cambridge, Mass.: Harvard University Press, 1967, 142–144.

Riemann, G. F. B. (1867). "On the Representability of a Function by Means of a Trigonometric Series" in Hawking, S. God Created the Integers, trans. Mireille Ansaldi. Philadelphia: Running Press, 2005, 826–865.

Riemann, G. F. B. (1868). On the hypotheses which lie at the foundation of geometry in From Kant to Hilbert: A Source Book in the Foundations of Mathematics, ed. Ewald, W. B., 2 vols. Oxford: Oxford University Press, 1996, 652–661.

Riemann, G. F. B. (1959). "On The Number of Prime Numbers Less Than a Given Quantity", (Berlin Academy), in Hawking, S. God Created the Integers, trans. J. Anders. Philadelphia: Running Press, 2005, 876–885.

Robinson, S. (2002). M. C. Escher: More Mathematics Than Meets The Eye." SIAM News 35, no. 8 (October).

Ronan, M. (2008). Multi-Dimensional Lives–Review on Marcus du Sautoy: Finding Moonshine: A Mathematician's Journey through Symmetry. Nature 451 (February 7) 629.

Rong Pan; Qiang Yang; Sinno Jialin Pan. (2007). Mining Competent Case Bases for Case-Based Reasoning. Artificial Intelligence 171, 1039–1068.

Rorty, R. (1979). Philosophy and the Mirror of Nature. Princeton, N.J.: Princeton University Press,

Rorty, R. (1982). Consequences of Pragmatism. Minneapolis: University of Minnesota Press.

Rorty, R. (1989). Contingency, Irony, and Solidarity. Cambridge: Cambridge University Press.

Rorty, R. (1991). Objectivity, Relativism, and Truth–Philosophical Papers, Volume 1. Cambridge: Cambridge University Press.

Rorty, R. (1998). Truth and Progress–Philosophical Papers, Volume 3. New York: Cambridge University Press.

Rorty, R. (2000). Philosophy and Social Hope. New York: Penguin.

Rorty, R. (2007). Philosophy as Cultural Politics. Cambridge: Cambridge University Press.

Russel, B. (1945). History of Western Philosophy, New York: Simon & Schuster, London.

Russel, B., Whitehead A. N. (1910–1913). Principia Mathematica, 3 vols., Cambridge: Cambridge University Press.

Svami Satya Prakash Sarasvati (1986). Founders of Sciences in Ancient India, 2 vols. New Delhi: Research Institute of Ancient Scientific Studies, New Delhi.

Savage, L. J. (1954). The Foundations of Statistics, NewYork: John Wiley.

Schelling, T. C. (1960). The Strategy of Conflict, Cambridge, Mass.: Harvard University Press.

Scholes, M. S., Black, F. (1973). The Pricing of Options and Corporate Liabilities. Journal of Political Economy 81, no. 3, 637–654.

Selman, B. (2008). A Hard Statistical View. Nature 451 (February), 639–640.

Seneca, L. A. (1972). Seneca in Ten Volumes. Trans. Basore, J. W., Corcoran, T. H. and R. M. Gummere, Miamisburg, Ohio: F. J. Miller.

Sextus Empiricus (1933-1949). Opera. ed. Mutschmann, H. and I. Man, Lepzig, 1912-1954.

Trans. Bury, R.G., Cambridge, Mass.: Harvard University Press, Loeb Classical Library, 1933-1949.

Sextus Empiricus. (2000). Outlines of Scepticism. 2nd ed., eds. Annas, J. and J. Barnes: Cambridge Texts in the History of Philosophy. New York: Cambridge University Press.

Shafarevich, I. R. (2005). Basic Notions of Algebra, trans. Miles Reid. Encl. Of Math. Sci. 11, Berlin: Springer.

Shafer, G. (1976). A Mathematical Theory of Evidence. Princeton: Princeton University Press,

Shafer, G. (1986). Probability judgement in artificial intelligence. In Uncertainty in Artificial Intelligence, eds. Kanal, L. N. and J. F. Lemmer, Amsterdam: Elsevier, 127-135.

Shafer, G., Logan, R. (1987). Implementing Dempster's Rule for Hierarchical Evidence. Artificial Intelligence 33, 271-298.

Shafer, G., Lindley, D. V., Spiegelhalter, D. J. (1987) Uncertainty in Expert Systems—discussion. Statistical Science 2 (1987): 3-44.

Shaohua Kevin Zhou; Rama Chellappa. (2006). From Sample Similarity to Ensemble Similarity: Probabilistic Distance Measures in Reproducing Kernel Hilbert Space. IEEE Trans. On Pattern Analysis and Machine Intelligence 28, no. 6 (June), 917-929.

Sharot, T., Riccardi, M.A., Raio, C. M., Phelps, E.A. (2007). Neural Mechanisms Mediating Optimism Bias. Nature 450 (November), 102-105.

Shermer, M. (2008). Sacred Science—Can Emergence Break The Spell of Reductionism And Put Spirituality back into Nature? Scientific American (July), 22.

Shor, P. W. (1994). Algorithms for quantum computation: Discrete logarithms and factoring. in Proc. 35nd Annual Symposium on Foundations of Computer Science, ed. Goldwasser, S. (IEEE Computer Society Press), 124-134.

Skolem, T. A. (1920). Logico-combinatorial investigations in the satisfiability or provability of mathematical propositions: A simplified proof of a theorem by Loewenheim in From Frege to Gödel: A Source Book in Mathematical Logic, 1879– 1931, ed. van Heijenoort, J., Cambridge, Mass.: Harvard University Press, 1967, 252-63.

Skolem, T. A. (1922). Some remarks on axiomatized set theory in From Frege to Gödel: A Source Book in Mathematical Logic, 1879– 1931, ed. van Heijenoort, J., Cambridge, Mass.: Harvard University Press, 1967, 290–301.

Skolem, T. A. (1923). The foundations of elementary arithmetic in From Frege to Gödel: A Source Book in Mathematical Logic, 1879– 1931, ed. van Heijenoort, J., Cambridge, Mass.: Harvard University Press, 1967, 302–333.

Skolem, T. A. (1928). On mathematical logic in From Frege to Gödel: A Source Book in Mathematical Logic, 1879– 1931, ed. van Heijenoort, J., Cambridge, Mass.: Harvard University Press, 1967, 508–524.

Smullyan, R. (1978). What is the Name of This Book? The Riddle of Dracula and Other Logical Puzzles. Englewood Cliffs, N.J.: Prentice-Hall.

Smullyan, R. (2001). Gödel's Incompleteness Theorems in The Blackwell Guide to Philosophical Logic, ed. Goble, L. Hoboken, N.J.: Wiley-Blackwell.

Spinoza, B. (1925-1987). Spinoza Opera, 5 vols. ed. Gebhardt, C. Heidelberg: Carl Winters, 1925, 1972, volume 5: 1987.

Spinoza, B. (1985). Ethics, ed. Gebhardt, C. In The Collected Writings of Spinoza, vol. 1, trans. Edwin Curley. Princeton: Princeton University Press.

Spinoza, B. (2001). Theological-Political Treatise, ed. Gebhardt, C., trans. Samuel Shirley, 2nd ed. Indianapolis: Hackett Publishing.

Stalnaker, R. (1980) A note on non-monotonic modal logic. Unpublished note, referred to in Thayse, A., ed., 1988. From Standard Logic to Logic Programming. Chichester: Wiley

Steinke, F., Schölkopf, B. (2008). Kernels, Regularization and Differential Equations." Pattern Recognition 41, 3271–3286.

Stewart, I. (2007). Some assembly needed. Nature 448 (July 26), 419.

Tarski, A. (1986). The Collected Papers of Alfred Tarski, 4 vols. Givant, S. R., and R. N. McKenzie, eds. Basel: Birkhauser.

Tarski, A. (1941). Introduction to Logic And to The Methodology of Deductive Sciences. Mineola, N.Y.: Dover Publications, 1994.

Tarski, A. (1944). The Semantical Concept of Truth and the Foundations of Semantics. Philosophy and Phenomenological Research 4, 341–375.

Tarski, A. (1956). Logic, Semantics, Metamathematics. Oxford: Clarendon Press.

Tarski, A. (1969). Truth and Proof. Scientific American 220, 63–77.

Terentius Maurus (1864). De Literis, Syllabis et Metris in: Grammatici Latini, ed. Keil, H. vol.6. Leipzig: Brockhaus, 313–413.

Thayse, A., ed. (1988). From Standard Logic to Logic Programming. Chichester: Wiley.

Turing, A. M. (1936). On computable numbers, with an application to the Entscheidungsproblem. Proc. London Mathematical Society Series 2, 42, 230–265.

Turing, A. M. (1937). Computability and lambda-definability. Journal of Symbolic Logic, 2 ,153-163.

Turing, A. M. (1950). Computing machinery and intelligence. Mind 59, 443-460.

Vamos, T. (1991). Computer Epistemology. Singapore: World Scientific

Vapnik, V. N. (2000). The Nature of Statistical Learning Theory. Information Science and Statistics. 2nd ed. New York: Springer.

Venn, J. (1866). The Logic of Chance, London: Macmillan.

Viète, F. (1591). In artem analyticam isagoge. Tours. In English: The Analytic Art, trans. T. Richard Witmer. Kent, Ohio: The Kent State University Press, 1983.

Vitruvius, P. (1960). The Ten Books on Architecture. Trans. Morris Hicky Morgan. Mineola, N.Y.: Courier Dover Publications.

Waerden, B.L. van der. (1993). Algebra I-II,: Springer, 1993, 2006.

Waerden, B. L. van der. (1985). A History of Algebra: From Al-Khwarizmi to Emmy Noether Berlin: Springer, 1985.

Walpole, H. (1965). in Serendipity and the Three Princes, from the Peregrinaggio of 1557, ed. Remer, T. G. with an Introduction and Notes; Preface by Lewis, W. S. Norman, Oklahoma: University of Oklahoma Press, 1965.

Wang, P. (2007). Three fundamental misconceptions of artificial intelligence. Journal of Experimental and Theoretical Artificial Intelligence 19, no. 3 (September), 249-268.

Weber, M (1904). Die protestantische Ethik und der Geist des Kapitalismus, Archiv für Sozialwissenschaften und Sozialpolitik, Bd. XX und XXI, Tübingen: Mohr Verlag, 1904 und 1905. In English: The Protestant Ethic And The Spirit of Capitalism. trans. Talcott Parsons/intro. Anthony Giddens. London: Routledge, 1992.

Weinberg, S. (2003). Facing up And Its Cultural Adversaries. Cambridge, Mass.: Harvard University Press.

Whitfield, J. (2005). Order out of Chaos. Nature 436 (18 August), 905-07.

Wigner, J. (1960) The Unreasonable Effectiveness of Mathematics in The Natural Sciences. Communications in Pure and Applied Mathematics 13, No. 1 (February), 1-14.

Williams, B. J., Jorge y Jorge, M. C. (2008). Aztec Arithmetic Revisited: Land-Area Algorithms and Acolhua Congruence Arithmetic. Science 320 (April 4), 72-77.

Wittgenstein, L. (1956). Tractatus logico-philosophicus. London: Routledge and Kegan Paul..

Young, J. Y. (1956). Visual Response by Octopus to Crabs and Other Figures before and after Training." J. of Experimental Biology 33, 709-729.

Zadeh, L. (1965). Fuzzy sets and systems in System Theory, ed. J. Fox (Brooklyn, N.Y.: Polytechnic Press, 29–39.

Zemanek, H. (1991). Weltmacht Computer, Weltreich der Information. Esslingen: Bechtle Verlag.

Zermelo, E. F. (1904). Proof That Every Set Can Be Well-Ordered in: From Frege to Gödel: A Source Book in Mathematical Logic, 1879–1931, ed. van Heijenoort, J., Cambridge, Mass.: Harvard University Press, 1967, 139–141.

Zermelo, E. F. (1908). A New Proof of The Possibility of Well-Ordering in: From Frege to Gödel: A Source Book in Mathematical Logic, 1879–1931, ed. van Heijenoort, J., Cambridge, Mass.: Harvard University Press, 1967, 183–198.

Zermelo, E .F. (1908). Investigations in The Foundations of Set Theory in: From Frege to Gödel: A Source Book in Mathematical Logic, 1879–1931, ed. van Heijenoort, J., Cambridge, Mass.: Harvard University Press, 1967, 199–215.

AI Magazine 26, no. 4 (2005)
AI Magazine 30, no. 3 (2009)
Artificial Intelligence 171, no. 18 (December 2007)–Special Review Issue
IEEE Annals of the History of Computing, quarterly, from 1979
Proof and Beauty. The Economist, April 2, 2005, p. 69–70.

Picture Credits

The author would like to thank Édua Szűcs for the cartoons; László Pal-kovics, for the pictures of Appendix 1.1; József Váncza, Márton Drótos, Gábor Erdős, Tamás Kis, for the text of Appendix 1.2; Barnabás Takács and Dávid Hanák for the results and faces; Gábor Renner; György Kovács; and Imre Paniti, for the manufacturing example of 2.4.3.

p. 26   Courtesy of Imre Paniti, SZTAKI, EU 6th FW Programme: SCULPTOR project (No. 0140269). CIM Research Laboratory, Computer and Automation Institute, Hungarian Academy of Sciences.

pp. 59, 62, 173   In Penrose, 2004.

p. 67   http://commons.wikimedia.org/wiki/Image: Transformation_ (before).png

p. 68   Courtesy of Digital Elite Inc., Los Angeles / Mary L. Carter, FunIcons: http://www.digitalelite.us.com/Pages/Digi-talElite/FunIcons.html

p. 76   www.phys.unsw.edu.au/PHYSICS/FRACTAL

p. 137   geosmart.wordpress.com, www.fortunecity.com

pp. 152-153   Courtesy of Prof. L. Palkovics, research director of the Knorr–Bremse Company, from his inaugural lecture as Member of the Hungarian Academy of Sciences.

p. 154   Courtesy of S.R. Kumara, presentation of the keynote paper Monostori, L.; Váncza, J.; Kumara, S.R.T.: Agent-based systems for manufacturing. CIRP Annals - Manufacturing Technology, 55(2), 697-720, (2006)

p. 158   http://weblog.fortnow.com

pp. 159, 189   http://goodmath.blogspot.com

p. 167   www.cs.sunysb.edu/~algorith/files/graph-isomorphism.
                shtml

p. 169   www-esd.lbl.gov, www.freepatentsonline.com

p. 172   cph-theory.persiangig.com/1190-5.jpg

Name Index

Subject Index